BEYOND THE GOD DELUSION

How Radical Theology
Harmonizes Science and Religion

Richard Grigg

FORTRESS PRESS
MINNEAPOLIS

BEYOND THE GOD DELUSION

For Drew and Hannah,
exemplary explorers

Library of Congress Cataloging-in-Publication Data

Grigg, Richard, 1955–
 Beyond the God delusion : how radical theology harmonizes science and religion / Richard Grigg.
   p. cm.
 ISBN-13: 978–0–8006–6272–1 (alk. paper)
 ISBN-10: 0–8006–6272–5 (alk. paper)
 1. Religion and science. 2. Theology. I. Title.
 BL240.3.G76 2007
 215—dc22   2007036579

The paper used in this publication meets the minimum requirements of American National Standard for Information Sciences — Permanence of Paper for Printed Library Materials, ANSI Z329.48-1984.

Manufactured in the U.S.A.

12   11   10   09   08   2   3   4   5   6   7   8   9   10

CONTENTS

ACKNOWLEDGMENTS

I must begin by thanking Professor Dennis Bielfeldt, who first put me on to some of the main issues in the relationship between science and religion, such as the potential conflict between conservation of energy and divine action in the world.

As always, thanks go also to my colleagues in the Department of Philosophy and Religious Studies at Sacred Heart University. They are, with annoying exceptions—you know who you are—delightful friends and supportive fellow-scholars. The New Haven Theology Group read an early version of chapter one and provided most helpful comments.

Finally, I don't underestimate the importance of having thoughtful friends who, from time to time, simply ask, "How's the book coming along?" This category of support includes comments that help one keep the proper perspective, such as my friend Grace's observation that writing a book can't count as "real work," given that it is a task that can be performed in one's pajamas.

INTRODUCTION

The story of science and religion begins in the seventeenth century when science as we know it came to birth, thanks to the
efforts of persons such as Galileo Galilei and Sir Isaac Newton.
All of us are familiar with the attack of the Christian church upon
Galileo. The church forced Galileo, under threat of torture, to
recant his claim that the earth revolved around the sun rather than
vice versa. And we know that conservative Christian churches
went on the warpath against Darwin's *Origin of the Species* once
they decided that it contradicted the biblical account of creation,
a course they continue to follow up to the present day. The most
famous of the creation-evolution clashes occurred two generations
after Darwin's theory, at the 1925 Scopes trial in Dayton, Tennessee, where a high school biology teacher (John Thomas Scopes)
was brought to court for teaching Darwin in his classroom. Such
high-profile incidents have led many to believe that science and
religion are naturally at odds, that the Christian scriptures, for
example, inevitably clash with the scientific worldview.[1]

Contemporary scholarship rejects the notion that there was
nothing but warfare between science and religion from the seventeenth century up to the dawn of the twentieth century. One need
only think, for instance, of the attitude of the great nineteenth-
century theologian John Henry Cardinal Newman, who believed
that science and religion had entirely separate concerns and, thus,
Darwinian evolution posed no threat to Christian belief. Indeed,
Newman's strategy for reconciling science and religion—science
and religion are engaged in two entirely different tasks and,
therefore, cannot collide—became the majority position among

mainline Christian theologians during the bulk of the twentieth century.[2] Many twentieth-century scientists embraced a parallel strategy, preferring to be tight-lipped: it was better to say nothing at all, to let sleeping dogs lie as if they were, in fact, asleep, lest those conservative Christians who still saw science as an enemy succeeded in having research funds cut off.

Today, however, thanks to the annoyance caused by Intelligent Design Theory and the horrors of religious violence, unusually strident scientific voices are being raised that claim that religion is not, in fact, immune from scientific assault. What is more, these voices carry the claim that science can show that belief in God is a "delusion," and a dangerous one at that.

I take the term *delusion*, of course, from evolutionary biologist Richard Dawkins's *The God Delusion*.[3] One of the criticisms aimed at Dawkins and some of his cohorts is that their critique of belief in God—the sort of belief that I shall call traditional Christian theism—assaults straw men and steers clear of the most serious Christian theologians.[4] What about those theologians, then, who have refused both antagonism toward science and separation from it? What should we make of serious theists who have made sophisticated attempts to show that science and religion can actually be harmonized?

As early as 1885, the American Unitarian theologian Francis Abbott published his *Scientific Theism*.[5] This remarkable book appropriated the nineteenth century's infatuation with an evolutionary interpretation of reality as a whole (not simply of the evolution of terrestrial species, Darwin's focus). That infatuation is best represented by the then towering philosophical influence of Herbert Spencer. Abbott, substituting an "organic" model of the universe's evolution for Spencer's "mechanical" one, worked out in detail what he took to be a happy interdependence of theological and scientific worldviews.

The premier mid-twentieth-century example of attempted reconciliation is undoubtedly the work of Jesuit theologian and paleontologist Pierre Teilhard de Chardin.[6] Teilhard, like Abbott, believed the key was to embrace a broadly evolutionary perspective. He produced a highly speculative system that attempted to combine a scientific, evolutionary view of the universe with Christian faith:

the entire universe is evolving toward the "Omega Point," the unity of all things in God.

Toward the end of the twentieth century and on into the present, others joined the search for a way to put science and religion in fruitful dialogue, to tear down the fences as it were. Christian thinkers such as Ian Barbour, Arthur Peacocke, John Polkinghorne, Nancey Murphy, and John Haught have taken up the challenge of squaring a relatively traditional Christianity with the latest discoveries of contemporary science (although they obviously do not march in absolute lockstep with one another or with any one articulation of Christian orthodoxy).[7] The attempts by these theologians—some of them theologian-scientists—to square the gospel with everything from evolution to quantum physics have attracted plenty of public attention, and they have generated numerous conferences and publications.

What, so far, are the fruits of the most recent efforts? One must say, first of all, that these efforts are impressive. The contemporary thinkers mentioned above, for example, are no intellectual or scientific lightweights. They know their science, they know their theology, and their work can only be deemed sophisticated and insightful. That is not the same, however, as saying that their work has been successful. In chapter one, I will show why it has, in fact, been unsuccessful. That is, even after considering the most erudite theological attempts to harmonize theism and science, theism must still be judged, using Dawkins's provocative expression, a delusion. But the point of the present book is not simply to second Dawkins's desultory conclusion. Rather, my fundamental thesis is that it is, in fact, possible for genuine friendship to be achieved between religion and science.

For that to happen, however, we need to make room at the table for a voice that has thus far been absent from the science-religion conversation. We need to consider what a *radical* brand of theology and spirituality might possibly contribute to the dialogue. The goal of my exploration, in other words, is neither to defend belief in God against scientific attack nor to use science as a tool with which to destroy religion. It is, rather, to rethink religion or spirituality (I shall use the two concepts interchangeably) so that it not only becomes fully compatible with natural science but also actually benefits from the scientific worldview. In order for this result to happen, we need, first of all, to make a conceptual leap beyond traditional Abrahamic theism. That conceptual leap can then become the basis for a practical transformation in spirituality.

Of course, terms such as *traditional theism, radical theology*, and even *science* can be problematic: they can each stand for a host of tendencies. We are inevitably reduced to using such terms as a form of shorthand, leaving unremarked countless possible qualifications. That does not mean, however, that we must employ such terms without any precision whatsoever. Here at the outset, we ought to provide some basic definitions. Traditional or mainline Christian theism,which overlaps significantly with various forms of Jewish and Muslim theism, begins with the conviction that there exists a God who is a transcendent personal consciousness who created the universe and who acts within that universe to preserve and guide it and to provide its sentient in habitants with salvation.By contrast, I shall define *radical theology* as a position that rejects the notion of a transcendent personal consciousness who created the world. Furthermore, though it may draw upon them as it sees fit, *radical theology* frees itself from subservience to traditional sources of authority such as the Bible, official church teachings and creeds, and the work of previous Christian thinkers.

The word *science* as used in this discussion will refer preeminently to the natural sciences, with physics and biology as paradigmatic examples. This should not be surprising, given that physics deals with that fundamental stratum of reality that religion and theology often wish to explore as well, and that so much of the controversy between religion and science has been over a biological issue, namely, the origin of the species.

Having considered the definition of *radical theology* offered here, one might well ask how such a position could count as a theology, having rejected the traditional God along with his familiar conduits of communication. The answer is that the sort of radical positions that we shall explore are philosophical refelections upon what deserves to be called the divine, and that is, of course, the task of theology. These reflections search for what is worthy of our ultimate devotion—that which has the best chance of fulfilling not just the individual's spiritual quest but also that which will assure the success of the whole human project and the well-being of the earth. Whatever is proposed to fill this role can be called "God" or "Goddess," with suitable caveats, if the individual radical thinker so chooses. Such a source of fulfillment takes on just that existential, practical role that traditions such as Judaism and Christianity have perennially identified with God.

The transition from traditional theism to what I am calling radical theology will entail a grasp of the difference between theism and pantheism. The term *theism* has already been defined above in the section on traditional theism. In contrast to theism, pantheism sees God not as a being separate from the rest of the universe, but as a power that is integral to it. Indeed, some forms of pantheism simply identify God with the universe taken as a whole. Other positions, sometimes termed *panentheism*, hold that God transcends the universe without being independent of it; the universe is one part of God's being. The brand of radical theology that will figure in our investigation will be a version of pantheism.

Chapter one lays out in detail the challenges that confront those who would harmonize science and traditional theism. Special attention is paid to the difficulty of squaring traditional notions of divine activity in the world with the scientific law of the conservation of mass-energy. Here we shall have a chance briefly to meet some of the most gifted and important advocates of harmonizing traditional Christian belief and contemporary science.

In chapter two we will confront what is, initially, problematic about the claim that radical theology can carry on a fruitful dialogue with natural science. There are four main difficulties to be considered, each of which may appear to undermine radical theology's claim to be a friend of science.

I will set forth in chapter three the argument that radical theologies can, in fact, be fruitfully, if not seamlessly, linked with the scientific perspective. To this end, I will briefly sketch the science-friendly positions of a number of contemporary radical religious thinkers. Then I will turn to a contemporary variety of pantheism, one focused on the physical universe uncovered by present-day natural science. This pantheism will be informed by the science-friendly radical theologies considered in the opening pages of the chapter. It will be my contention that it provides one model for an effectual blending of radical theology and science.

Chapter four considers what puts the unity in the universe. It goes on to ponder where a Christology might fit within a scientifically informed radical theology.

Chapter five plumbs some of the practical implications for spirituality that arise from linking radical theology and science. It shows how specific components of the contemporary scientific worldview can be taken up into radical theology so as to create a rewarding spirituality.

Chapter six inverts the discussion of the previous chapter. It asks what, if anything, radical theology can do for science. The chapter will argue that, while the scientific enterprise certainly does not *need* radical theology to do its scientific work, something can, indeed, be gained—even where science itself is concerned—by linking science and radical theology.

Finally, by way of conclusion, in chapter seven I provide a brief assessment of what I take to be the prospects for an alliance of radical theology with science. Does this alliance have a chance of being taken up by and of informing the worldview of a significant number of persons in the contemporary world?

Radical theology is in a significantly better position than traditional theism to reconcile science and religion. But quite apart from the question of exactly what the prospects are for a compact between radical theology and science in comparison to the future of more traditional scientifically informed theologies, it is surely desirable to add another voice to the conversation about religion and science. Radical theology is that other voice. After all, science and theology are both about inquiry, about putting all the effort we can muster into the endeavor to understand our world and our faith. And putting every effort into this project means listening to every voice that might have something to contribute. That is the spirit of science, as it is the spirit of "faith seeking understanding."[8]

CHAPTER ONE

An Experiment Gone Awry: Science and Traditional Theism

Some commentators would have us believe that there has been a sea change in the relationship between natural science and biblical religion. In the seventeenth through the nineteenth centuries, we are told, religion and science were at war with one another. A conflict symbolized by names such as Galileo, Laplace, and Darwin, raged. Yet, contemporary scholarship has questioned the severity of this warfare between science and religion and has pointed out that the human sciences and the historical-critical approach to the Bible probably caused more problems for Christian piety than did natural science.[1] Nonetheless, there can be little doubt, to cite but one example, that the classical Newtonian picture of a completely determined, machine-like universe presented serious challenges to traditional Christian beliefs. On the effects of Newton's view of the universe, consider Timothy Ferris' claim that "Newton saw science as a form of worship, yet Newtonian mechanics had a dolorous effect upon traditional belief in a Christian God."[2] (But note, too, theologian N. Max Wildiers' observation that Bonaventura and other medieval theologians had already compared the world to a gigantic machine.[3])

But the common wisdom among recent proponents of what was defined in the Preface as traditional theism seems to be that, whatever the character of the conflict between science and religion in an earlier cultural epoch, in our own contemporary milieu that conflict is a thing of the past; a genuine rapprochement is being achieved. The old deterministic scientific worldview, so hostile to notions of human freedom and divine action in the world, has given way to a wholly different scientific perspective, a perspective with which traditional religious commitments can readily be harmonized. The popular press has duly reflected this optimism: *Newsweek* emblazoned its cover with the words, "Science Finds God"; *The New York Times* headed an article "Science and Religion Cross Their Line in the Sand"; and Gregg Easterbrook, writing for *The Los Angeles Times*, announced that "the Big Bang is looking more supernatural all the time." *Wired*, a must-read periodical for the digitally up-to-date, provided a much more sober cover for its December 2002 issue: "Special Report: Science + Religion." But inside the magazine, Easterbrook once again took up his cheerleading duties with an article entitled "The New Convergence."[4]

It is my contention in this first chapter, however, that this now familiar optimism on the part of religious thinkers about the possibility of harmonizing science and classical Christian theism is premature at best. Indeed, it seems to me that biblical theism faces a crisis in its present confrontation with science. Until recently, one might have been excused for believing that such talk of a crisis contradicted the common wisdom not only of the progressive theological community, but of the scientific community as well. But, as indicated in the Preface, one of the extraordinary intellectual events of the first part of the twenty-first century is the sudden willingness of scientists, most notably Richard Dawkins, to voice their objections to traditional theism, and to do so in no uncertain terms.

My argument in this chapter is divided into two main parts. First, I shall suggest that the results of even the best current attempts by tradition-oriented Christian thinkers to render theology compatible with science on one crucial issue have come, at least up to this point, to naught. Second, I shall attempt to defeat the notion that science and religion are two wholly separate, incommensurable projects. This second part of my argument is as important as the first, for if science and religion were, indeed, entirely separate, then the failure of current attempts to render them compatible would be inconsequential; indeed, those attempts would be both unnecessary and naive. In both parts of this first chapter, I shall pay special attention to the problem of divine action in the world and to the role of the scientific principle of the conservation of energy in creating that problem.

Traditional Christian Thinkers' Contemporary Dialogue with Science

While it should be entirely obvious that the rise of the modern natural sciences has had important implications for traditions other than Christianity, I am self-consciously confining myself in this chapter to the Christian tradition's grappling with science. The phrase *traditional Christian thought*, or what I shall also call *traditional theism*, and sometimes *biblical theism*, may hit some as hopelessly vague. For my purposes here, however, it can be defined stipulatively, as indicated in the Preface, as belief in a transcendent personal consciousness who self-consciously acts within the world of nature that he has created. Of course, the fact that the definition is stipulative does not render it arbitrary: it is meant to pick out a particular perspective on God that is relevant to our present discussion and that is, in fact, embraced by a vast number of persons. It has long been recognized that this concept of God is bedeviled by internal conflicts. The primary source of those conflicts is the fact that the God of traditional Christian doctrine is the product of an uneasy synthesis. It puts together—or attempts to do so— the anthropomorphic, interventionist, eminently personal God of the Old Testament (the Jewish Bible) with the Greek philosophers' notion of ultimacy. The latter notion, far from suggesting a personal being who acts in history, tends to focus upon abstractions such as the "One," or pure "Being." When Moses asked God what his name was, and God replied, "I am that I am" (Exod. 3:14), most interpreters schooled in the thought-world of the Jewish Bible interpreted God's response as a wily refusal to give a name. But early Christian interpreters of the same passage almost immediately drew upon Greek philosophy and took the "I am" to mean that God is to be identified with Being. From the beginning of Christian history, then, the God of classical Christian theism has been an unstable construction.

Note also that, in the pages that follow, I speak interchangeably about "science and religion," "science and faith," and "science and theology." One can, of course, make terminological distinctions here. For example, faith is a function of existential commitment, while theology is a second-order theoretical analysis of that commitment and its object. But it should not be necessary to employ such distinctions here, inasmuch as the scientific worldview is problematic for religion and faith just to the degree that religion and faith are informed by some degree of theological reflection.

Contemporary theologians can hardly be blamed for hoping that something productive might come of a discussion with the most recent incarnations of natural science. It is surely beyond dispute that there have been shifts in science in the last one hundred years. First of all, the majority of those who philosophize about the scientific enterprise no longer conceive of science as built upon absolutely indubitable foundations and as leading to absolutely incontrovertible objective conclusions. Contemporary thinkers are more apt to theorize about science in terms of Willard Van Orman Quine's holist epistemology with its notion of the "web of belief" than in terms of Enlightenment foundationalism.[5] We can add to this the indeterminism that contemporary physics finds on the atomic and subatomic levels of reality and the claim by some philosophers of science that the history of science is not a matter of linear progress but involves frequent abandonment of previously sacrosanct paradigms in favor of something genuinely new. These shifts do make a difference for Christian theology. From the Enlightenment perspective, theology's claims to legitimacy looked dubious at best, given that theology could not point to the kind of indubitable empirical foundations that science supposedly possessed. But once it is recognized that no approach to reality, science included, rests upon the kind of secure foundations that Enlightenment thinkers were convinced propped up their thinking, then theology's claim to offer convincing justifications for religious beliefs can be taken with renewed seriousness.[6]

Perhaps the most significant change in the content of our scientific understanding of the universe is that the Newtonian picture of a completely determined macroscopic world has been augmented by the notorious claim that quantum indeterminacy reigns on the micro level. But it is here, with regard to shifts in the specific content of the scientific worldview, that theologians are most apt to exaggerate, if not simply to fall into confusion. For one thing, the real degree and import of these changes in scientific thinking are unclear. Timothy Ferris points out, for example, that well-established theories, though they may turn out to be subsets of larger

> and farther-reaching ones—as happened when Newtonian mechanics was incorporated by Einstein into general relativity—are seldom proved wrong. As the physicist Steven Weinberg writes, "One can imagine a category of experiments that *refute* well-accepted theories, theories that have become part of the standard consensus of physics. *Under this category, I can find no examples whatever in the past one hundred years.*"[7]

Of course, one might argue that in the last one hundred years there have been no instances of the refutation of a previously accepted theory because the ability to reweave Quine's "web of belief" allows science to hold onto old theories even when new and initially troubling evidence arises. The theories can be retained because other parts of the web are altered, or because the theories themselves are placed in a new context and interpreted in a different fashion. But the most relevant fact is that, however significant the change in the content of the scientific worldview, the present version of that worldview turns out, upon close scrutiny, still to pose serious challenges to traditional biblical theism. Of those various challenges, probably the most serious has to do with the problem of divine action in the world. Christian faith has ordinarily thought of God as interacting with the world both in order to preserve it and to alter its course from time to time. In the latter category falls subtle providential guidance as well as the possibility of dramatically visible interventions. But science has usually claimed that on the macro level, the level upon which human experience has purchase, the events that constitute the world are determined by the laws of nature, whatever the ontological status of those laws. This entails the conviction that all macro events can, at least in principle, be thoroughly explained by reference to natural causal principles.

God's Action and the Conservation of Energy

One of the most important of natural causal principles is the law of the conservation of energy: in a closed system, the total amount of energy must remain the same; energy can change form, but it cannot genuinely be created or destroyed. But then how can God be said to act in the world, for any divine action within the natural sphere would register as an illicit addition of energy, a violation of the law of the conservation of energy? In a pre-scientific age, Thomas Aquinas could invoke the notion of primary and secondary causality, according to which God is the prime cause who carries out his will in the world by acting through secondary causes. But for the notion of God acting through secondary causes to have any meaning, for it to suggest that something genuinely different would happen if God were not present in the process, then God must add something to the natural or "secondary" causes. In other words, it must make a difference that God is present. But any such difference would, so it seems, necessarily result in just that violation that needs to be avoided, for it would involve the importation of energy from outside the closed system of the universe.

A significant number of contemporary theologians, and of scientists who hold theological convictions, have been wrestling with this issue of late. Most modestly conceived, their project need not show how God does, in fact, act within the natural world without violating the principle of the conservation of energy, but only that there are consistent ways of understanding how God *might* do so. But my sense is that the participants in the science-theology dialogue have not fared well in their attempt to accomplish even this modest version of the task. A brief survey of the proposals of several important thinkers in the current discussion will indicate the difficulties in their various positions, positions that frequently serve to undermine one another.

Any attempt to reconcile the present-day scientific worldview with divine action will need to find a gap, not in our contemporary scientific understanding of the world, but in the natural causal framework of the world itself as it is understood in contemporary science. That framework, it will have to be argued, does not *exhaustively* determine the behavior of the world. There must be a place, a so-called "causal joint," where God can interface with the world and influence it without upsetting the natural causal framework. With respect to the law of the conservation of energy in particular, there must be an interface with the world where God can supply something that is in addition to the world's natural causal processes, but he must do so without adding energy to those processes. There are three scientific vantage points, in particular, from which theologians have recently suggested that we might spy the requisite gap: chaos theory, the notion of top-down or downward causation (both chaos theory and top-down causation are often connected with the idea of non-energetic information), and the theory of quantum indeterminacy. Some readers may be surprised that process theology does not take pride of place in the discussion that follows, since process theologians have for decades argued that the Whiteheadian metaphysic behind most versions of process thought is uniquely compatible with the contemporary scientific worldview. Ian Barbour, for example, is a thinker who has for many years been associated with the dialogue between science and religion and who has embraced the process perspective.[8] But as John Polkinghorne points out, while process thought may be *abstractly* compatible with science, it is "without obvious consonance with what we know about general physical process." He goes on to argue that "this absence of anchorage in physical science is only one difficulty. More significant theologically is the confining of divine interaction to a purely persuasive role."[9] But of most importance, what of the fact that most contemporary science has absolutely no interest in any form of panpsychism?[10] Be that as it may, we shall, in fact, have a chance to make a passing reference to process thought when we consider John Haught's theology of evolution, in that Haught will link process theology with the attempt to make use of non-energetic information in talking about divine action.

Chaos theory has been much discussed in recent decades, even in popular books and magazine articles. Chaotic systems exhibit what is termed "sensitive dependence on initial conditions." Thus, the slightest perturbation of those conditions can result in massive and wholly unpredictable changes in the system. Of the many examples that might be given of such a system, the most famous is the so-called "butterfly effect": the mere flapping of a butterfly's wings may, through a whole concatenation of events much too difficult for us to trace, result in a large storm in a distant part of the world.

For John Polkinghorne, a Professor of Mathematical Physics at Cambridge University who is also an Anglican priest and one of the best known participants in the present science and religion discussion, chaotic systems provide an opening for divine action. Polkinghorne explains our inability to predict the future states of chaotic systems as more than just the result of the limitations of our knowledge. He suggests that there is in these systems themselves an openness, a degree of indeterminacy, such that the ordinary causal principles at work—"the interchange of energy between the isolable constituent parts of a physical system"—do not wholly determine the future of the system.[11] Two chaotic systems that are at one point virtually identical to one another can end up being vastly different. And this hints at the possibility of an additional causal influence, that is an influence distinguishable from the causal principles at work between the isolable parts that make up the system. What is more, Polkinghorne believes that this additional influence can be conceived to operate not by adding extra energy to the system, but simply by adding information:

> We know that situations which differ only infinitesimally in their initial circumstances (and so, effectively, *have the same energetic properties*) will nevertheless (because of the exponential enhancement of those differences) display different behaviors as they explore the pattern of future possibility open to them. It is natural to consider these infinitesimal differences that determine what actually occurs as akin to *"informational input,"* selecting a particular pattern of exploration.[12]

The payoff here, for Polkinghorne, is that God can be conceived as operating within chaotic systems through a "holistic" causality, an "informational causality" that does not disturb the natural causal interactions among the constituent elements of the system or violate the law of the conservation of energy.[13]

But the fatal flaw in Polkinghorne's argument is the fashion in which he moves from epistemology to ontology and claims that our inability to predict in detail the future states of a chaotic system is a function of a genuine openness or indeterminacy within the system itself. Strictly speaking, Polkinghorne does not hold that the system is wholly indeterminate, but that the "bottom-up" causality that obtains among the isolable parts of the system does not exhaust the causal influences at work within the system. Thus, the system has an element of indeterminacy as causal determination is ordinarily understood. But the orthodox scientific interpretation of chaotic systems is that they are thoroughly deterministic. It is simply that the causal processes at work in those systems are too complicated for us to trace. Thus, Nancey Murphy, who is in many other respects Polkinghorne's fellow-traveler theologically, explains that

> the grounds upon which chaos theorists argue for the unpredictability of future states depend upon the assumption that the future states *are determined by* the initial conditions in so sensitive a manner that we cannot measure them. So the systems are presumed to be determined at a very precise level—small changes *produce* large effects.[14]

As Murphy explains, we must distinguish here "between predictability (an epistemological concept) and causal determinism (an ontological concept)." She points out, furthermore, that even if Polkinghorne's notion of an element of indeterminacy within chaotic systems were valid, it is not at all clear how God could act within this gap. Polkinghorne suggests that God might act via a non-energetic contribution of information. "But," asks Murphy, "to whom or what is the information contributed? How is it conveyed without any energy at all"?[15] Yet, another problem is that recent investigations have suggested that truly chaotic systems in nature are rarer than once thought. Hence, even if God could act in the world through chaotic systems, they would afford him few opportunities for action.

God and Top-Down Causality

What, then, of the second approach to which contemporary theological commentators on science and religion call our attention, namely, top-down causality? The notion of top-down causality is based upon the kind of whole-part relationship in which the whole is greater than the sum of the parts. What advocates of top-down causality must show, specifically, is that the whole has a causal impact upon its constituent elements that, while not independent of the "bottom-up" causal interactions among those elements, is nonetheless distinguishable from them. This scenario appears to hold out the possibility of non-energetic causal efficacy: while the whole has a causal influence upon its parts, it adds no energy to those parts.

Let us consider a specific example from the realm of living organisms, an example originally set forth by Donald Campbell but brought to bear on the problem of divine action by Arthur Peacocke.[16] If one considers the jaw structure of a single worker termite on the molecular level, one focuses on the particular proteins out of which the jaw is made and how the DNA sequences in the termite's cells have led to the production of those proteins. What we observe on this micro level can be explained in terms of the causal interactions among the individual molecular components or parts of the termite. This is an example of bottom-up causality. But the larger structure of the termite's jaw—the whole rather than the individual parts—helps determine the termite's chances of success in attaining food and, hence, its chances of surviving and passing on its genetic material in reproduction. But this means that the larger structure of the jaw, the macro-level, acts back upon the molecular or micro-level where later members of the species are concerned. The DNA of those later members of the species will be selected on the basis of the strengths and weaknesses of various jaw configurations. The jaw of the termite, or the jaw along with the environment in which the termite must attempt to survive, thus appears to have a top-down effect upon the molecular level.

How does the macro level exercise its influence on the micro level here? Peacocke's argument returns us to the notion of non-energetic information:

> We seem . . . to have here a determination of form through a *flow of information*, as distinct from a transmission of energy, where "information" is conceived of in a broad enough sense to include the selective input from the environment towards molecular structures—for example, the DNA sequences in the termite jaw example.[17]

Peacocke thinks in terms of a hierarchy of systems, in which the higher systems have top-down causal effects upon the lower. God-and-the-universe is the most complex system, and in his position at the very top of the hierarchy, God can exercise non-energetic top-down causal influence upon the rest of the universe.

In the succinct formulation of an advocate of top-down causality, "we invoke the concept of top-down causation when we find processes that *cannot be described or understood* in abstraction from the whole system, comprised of the affected entity in its environment."[18] And this brings us to a possible flaw in the notion of top-down causation parallel to what we discovered in the attempt to read chaotic systems as non-deterministic: there may well be an unwarranted leap from epistemic limitations to ontological claims. Dennis Bielfeldt has shown the specific fashion in which the concept of downward causation arises out of *"perspectival, epistemic and explanatory limitation".[19]*

> Suppose it is the case that certain micro-physical properties instantiate the higher-level property of being an ant jaw. Suppose further, that with this jaw the ant can acquire the food and reproduction necessary to change the DNA encoding producing the jaw. Have we shown that the "higher level" jaw (and the subsequent macro-events it triggers) downwardly affects the distribution of the micro-physical? The critical question pertains to the ontological status of the higher-level properties. For instance, if the jaw is instantiated by DNA properties, then the use of the jaw in acquiring food is also instantiated by lower-level properties. By extension, the reproduction and selection that changes the lower-level properties is itself instantiated by lower-level properties. But if this is so, the "feedback"

does not in principle require a leap to a higher level, but rather is traceable by remaining at the level of the micro-physical. . . . Of course, we tend to want to think in downward terms because our theories of natural selection quantify over macro-physical events and entities. . . . The illusion of downward causality occurs when we seek to join the entities and events of a macro-physical theory to the entities and events of the micro-physical. It is because we are *epistemically limited* in specifying the events and entities realizing the macro-physical theory that we resort to downward causality.[20]

Bielfeldt's analysis short-circuits the notion of top-down causation by showing how, if our knowledge of the micro-physical level were sufficient, we could close the causal loop at that level. Neurologist Joseph LeDoux provides parallel evidence. The brain's working memory is, in simplest terms, formed by synaptic connections that are created thanks to sensory input from the external world that comes, for example, through vision. But working memory, discharging its "executive function," can then act back upon its building blocks, such as visual stimuli, by controlling what we attend to and what we see. LeDoux happily terms this *downward causation*. But, as he explains, "Downward causation is only mind-boggling if you believe that thoughts are one phenomenon and brain activities another." But they are, in fact, not separate phenomena. Both the bottom-up formation of working memory and the downward action of working memory on how we see the world are simply a matter of synaptic connections in the brain. Both can be analyzed in synaptic terms so that there is nothing causally mysterious and non-energetic about the brain's downward causation.[21]

Where Is God in the System?

But even if we were to bracket this possible flaw in the concept of top-down causality and assume, for the sake of argument, that the concept is valid, it would not help us to understand God's action in the world. Once again, Nancey Murphy provides an effective critique of her fellow theist. She does accept the notion of top-down causation. Murphy holds that it is of crucial importance in understanding, for example, how the human subject, dependent as it is upon the natural causal processes of the human brain, exhibits a consciousness that has causal powers of its own, powers that can freely be directed back upon the same natural processes out of which consciousness arises. (Note, however, that, at least in her initial response to Bielfeldt's critiques of top-down causality, she is unable to mount a substantive rejoinder to Bielfeldt's position, which also would leave her, one presumes, without an answer to LeDoux.)[22] But she admits, with a nod to Peacocke's work, that top-down causation is problematic when applied to God's relationship to the world. "The clearest account given so far of how God operates," explains Murphy, "is by *analogy* to human (top-down) agency in the inanimate world." The human person is a complex reality that emerges from the interaction of entities and processes on the prehuman level, yet the person can choose to act back upon that lower level of reality. "However, this analogy does not solve the problem because human agency is brought to bear on the natural world via bodily action. Since God has no body, we get no help with the question of *how* God brings it about that events obey his will."[23]

Again, the concept of top-down causality is used to explain systems in which an entity is affected by a larger whole of which it is a part, such as a living organism in an environment. However,

> in such cases, it appears that the effect of the environment is always mediated by specific changes in the entity itself. For example, team spirit only affects an individual insofar as sights and sounds emanating from the other people affect the individual's sensory organs. Environmental factors affect individual organisms by means of, say, food surpluses or shortages, which in turn affect an animal only insofar as it does or does not eat. So top-down causation by God should also be expected to be mediated by specific changes in the affected entities, and this returns us to the original question of how and at what level of organization God provides causal input into the system.[24]

Peacocke himself seems to be alluding to a similar problem when he acknowledges that

> in the world we observe through the sciences, we know of no transfers of information without some exchange of matter and/or energy, however minimal. So to speak of God as "informing" the world-as-a-whole [that is, of God guiding the world] without such inputs of matter/energy (that is, as not being "intervention") is but to accept the ultimate, ontological gap between the nature of God's own being and that of the created world, all-that-is-apart from God.[25]

Translation: transfer of information does, in fact, always involve expenditure of energy. Oxford scientist David Deutsch, who played a large part in opening the topic of quantum computing, is admirably concrete, concentrating on the matter side of the matter-energy equation: "Ultimately, information has to have a physical realization; that's why it does come down to atoms or stars or whatever in the end."[26] What is more, the notion of God adding information to the universe violates not only the law of the conservation of energy, instantiated in the first law of thermodynamics, but the second law of thermodynamics as well! As physicist Victor Stenger points out, "Information is equivalent to entropy, or at least changes in entropy. Thus, God's intervention by the injection of information would amount to a violation of the second law of thermodynamics, with all the entropy of a process not accounted for within our universe."[27] The entropy of a system is its relative amount of disorder. Adding information to a system changes the balance of order and disorder within it. If God were to add information to a natural system, then God would upset the natural balance. Hence, the information-as-causality model of God's action in the world does not really help us to escape violation of the conservation law at all.

This conclusion is a disappointing one, not just for thinkers such as Peacocke and Polkinghorne, but also for readers of John Haught's elegant treatments of how Christian theology ought to approach Darwinian evolution.[28] Evolution is, after all, one of the oldest sources of contention, for some, between Christianity and science. The question of God and evolution is, as Haught's work indicates, a specific instance of the question we are now debating, namely, how God can act in the world. For what the progressive Christian theologian such as Haught wants to be able to claim is that, while evolution proceeds according to the principles of random variation and natural selection laid out by Darwin, there is still a role for God in guiding this process. God has to be able to act here if evolution is not to be a thoroughly non-teleological process and human life simply a "glorious accident," as Stephen Jay Gould wonderfully put it.[29] Haught's proposal, based on the philosophies of Alfred North Whitehead and Pierre Teilhard de Chardin, is that God does not crudely reach into the physical world and alter the evolutionary process, but rather that God "lures" it forward, offering it various possibilities. God draws evolution along, specifically, through non-energetic information. But we have seen that, when it comes to the matter of divine action in the world, the information-as-causality position violates both the first and the second laws of thermodynamics, namely, the law of the conservation of energy and the law of entropy.

Frederick Crews, perhaps best known for debunking the more outrageously unscientific aspects of Freudian theory, writes that John Haught

> relocates God in the future and depicts him not as a planner but as "a transcendent force of attraction." But it doesn't occur to Haught that such teleology is just what Darwin managed to subtract from science. Whether pushing us or pulling us toward his desired end, the Christian God is utterly extraneous to evolution as Darwin and his modern successors have understood it. Evolution is an undirected, reactive process—the opposite of Haught's construal—or nothing at all.[30]

Hence, the problem of the conservation of energy aside, the information-as-causality avenue to interpreting evolution fundamentally misunderstands what evolution is all about.

God and Indeterminacy

We have seen Nancey Murphy's reactions to some of her colleagues' attempts to deal with divine action. Her own solution to the problem brings us to the third main topic that must be considered here, quantum indeterminacy. If God's interaction with his creation cannot be understood in top-down terms, then we must consider bottom-up causation. And the very bottom of the bottom-up causal structure of the universe is the quantum level. The behavior of quantum particles is notoriously indeterminate:

> Now, the peculiarity of entities at the quantum level is that while specific particles have their distinguishing characteristics and specific possibilities for acting, it is not possible to predict *exactly when* they will do whatever they do. . . . The question is what induces them to take one course of action rather than the other (or to take a course of action at a particular time rather than another or not at all).[31]

In contrast to chaotic systems, however, our inability to predict the precise future states of particular quantum particles is not simply a function of epistemic limitations that prevent us from tracing fully the causal network that applies on the quantum level. Rather, there is a genuine indeterminacy within quantum reality itself. And, for Murphy, this gap in the deterministic structure at the bottom of the physical world presents an opening for divine influence. "My proposal," she explains, "is that God's governance at the quantum level consists in activating or actualizing one or another of the quantum entity's innate powers at particular instants, and that these events are not possible without God's action."[32] Or, "to put it crudely, God is the hidden variable."[33] By influencing events at the absolutely basic quantum level, God can influence all that occurs in the universe since everything in the universe is ultimately rooted in quantum reality. What is more, that influence should be non-energetic and, hence, immune from the charge that it violates the conservation law. Indeterminate quantum processes, such as the movement of a particular electron or the sudden decay of a neutron, are at the very rock-bottom foundations of physical reality; there is nothing external to them causing them to occur. If there were physical causes, energy would be required to activate the quantum phenomena. But with genuine indeterminacy, that is, a complete lack of causal influence, there is no expenditure of energy in the initiation of the event (though the event itself may result in energy expenditure, as when an electron's leap from a higher orbit to a lower one results in the emission of a photon). Biologist Kenneth Miller makes a proposal similar to Murphy's: "The indeterminate nature of quantum events would allow a clever and subtle God to influence events in ways that are profound, but scientifically undetectable to us."[34]

Quantum reality currently provides the most promising avenue to thinking about divine action. Yet, there are still contentious issues that must be confronted. First of all, it is not entirely clear how God's manipulation of quantum states, states that *in the statistical aggregate are regular and predictable*, can actually help shape macro events, events on the level perceptible to human beings, for example. Some commentators contend that any quantum tweaking that God might perform would be overwhelmed by the statistical regularity of quantum events taken en masse. Hence, Jeffrey Koperski concludes, "Random quantum events are washed out in the macroscopic realm and cannot serve as a foundation for a sufficiently rich model of divine agency."[35] Murphy herself confesses,

> The most serious weakness of this paper is in describing the consequences of the theory of divine action at the quantum level for events at the macro-level. What, exactly, are the possibilities for God's determining the outcomes of events at the macro-level by governing the behavior of sub-atomic entities?[36]

And elsewhere she writes, in what critics might deem resignation, "I have to leave it to the physicists to argue over the relations between the micro and macro levels."[37]

Some writers do, however, take an optimistic view of the potential impact of individual quantum events on the macro level and, hence, of the promise of such events as openings for divine action. Robert John Russell contends, for example, that "the production of specific effects in the macroscopic level from quantum processes includes a whole range of phenomena such as the animal eye responding to a single photon, mental states resulting from quantum events at neural junctions, or the phenotypic expression of a single genetic mutation in an organism (resulting, for example, in sickle-cell anemia or cancer)."[38] We should note that the animal eye will respond to a single photon, however, only if all sorts of other conditions apply. For instance, if the animal is staring into bright light, the single photon will, I presume, have no independent causal effect.[39] Thus, before God could influence the world via single quantum events, he would have to be able to manipulate the extraordinarily complex macro-context in which the single quantum events take place. In this example, God would have to see to it that the animal was not, in fact, staring at the sunlight in front of it. And that fact, in essence, leaves us back where we began: just how could God accomplish these macro tasks?

The second potentially controversial issue affecting Murphy's proposal is connected with her claim that God's action is the hidden *determinant* in quantum processes. William Stoeger observes that Murphy and some other thinkers

> consider the indeterminacy at the quantum level to be an essential gap which requires filling. . . . my assessment is that indeterminacy is not a gap in this sense, but rather an expression of the fundamentally different physical character of reality at the quantum level. It does not need to be filled! To do so, particularly with divine intervention, would lead in my view to unresolvable scientific and theological problems. The demand for a cause to determine the exact position and time of an event misconstrues the nature of the reality being revealed. Quantum events need a cause and have a cause, but not a cause determining their exact time and position of occurrence, beyond what is specified by quantum probability (the wave function).[40]

If Stoeger's position is correct, and I believe that most scientists would say that it is—they hold that *it is the defining nature of quantum events that they are simply not determined*, not by God nor by any other hidden variable—then it appears that Murphy's project is doomed before it has even begun.

The major difficulty with the quantum proposal advanced by thinkers such as Nancey Murphy and Kenneth Miller, however, is that it too fails to avoid violation of the conservation law although that is precisely what it sets out to do. Quantum physicists view the quantum level as absolutely fundamental. Hence, there are no discrete causes antecedent to individual quantum events. Given this fact, it should perhaps be unsurprising, despite the notoriously counter-intuitive character of much quantum theory, that quantum events are indeterminate. If literally nothing precedes them in the world's causal networks, then quantum events must simply happen. Physicist Marcus Chown confirms this fact with exemplary economy: "It is a characteristic feature of quantum events that they happen randomly, for no reason at all."[41] And, since such events happen without a preceding reason, just how they happen cannot be predicted. Furthermore, their primal status means that quantum events are not the result of expenditures of energy causing them to occur.

What Murphy's proposal does, however, as she herself puts it, is to make God a hidden determinant in quantum processes. In other words, now there *is* something that precedes quantum events in the universe's causal networks, namely, divine action. But this means that the supposedly non-energetically caused, because absolutely bedrock, quantum events are no longer absolutely bedrock and thus no longer non-energetically caused. The confusion here is that, if we start with the recognition that quantum events occur without preceding expenditure of causal energy, then it seems that we should be able to attach God to the process and say that God is activating the events without introducing energy into the closed system of the physical universe. But adding God to the equation, in fact, changes the equation in just such a way as to make quantum events dependent upon antecedent energy expenditures. Hence, in this form at least, a proposal for understanding divine action in terms of quantum processes is no more successful in avoiding the second law of thermodynamics than are proposals based on top-down causation and chaos theory.

A Test Case: Prayer

It seems, then, as if the attempt to square the idea of God's action in the world with the scientific worldview is cut off at every pass. Indeed, suppose that we step back and consider the ultimate claim of divine action vis-a-vis the cosmos, namely, that God created the whole cosmos in the first place. That claim is, of course, absolutely central to traditional Christian (not to mention Jewish and Muslim) theism: "In the beginning . . . God created the heavens and the earth" (Gen. 1:1).[42] Yet there are fundamental components of contemporary physics that numerous scientists believe rule out the notion of a designer and creator of the universe. For example, the Big Bang can only be understood as operating on the quantum level where, as we have seen, *quantum uncertainty removes the notion of determination or cause.* Furthermore, the current search by physicists for a unified field theory, what might turn out to be a "theory of everything," has been gathering steam in recent decades. A goodly number of physicists are convinced that the much-publicized "string theory"[43] will soon provide such a theory of everything. But this theory might well turn out to show that the universe inevitably has the structure that it does; it could not have been otherwise. String advocate Brian Greene points out that this inevitability would have profound implications for

> some of the deepest questions of the ages. These questions emphasize the mystery surrounding *who or what made the seemingly innumerable choices apparently required to design our universe.* Inevitability answers these questions by erasing the options. Inevitability means that, in actuality, there are no choices. Inevitability declares that the universe could not have been different. No designer is required to make decisions about how to put the universe together.[44]

If all of these arguments about science and divine action seem a bit abstract, what about applying the scientific method itself to claims of divine action? Is there any arena in which actual empirical studies can be performed? The popular media has in recent years hyped news of studies purporting to show that piety and prayer can measurably improve human health. Sometimes, though, even the popular media can rise to the challenge of taking an objective look at something like religion and health. Thus, in a *Newsweek* article entitled "Faith and Healing," Claudia Kalb reviews the most careful scientific investigations of religion and health.[45] She reports that "Lynda H. Powell, an epidemiologist at Rush University Medical Center in Chicago, reviewed about 150 papers [on faith and healing] . . . . In one respect, her findings were not surprising: while faith provides comfort in times of illness, it does not significantly slow cancer growth or improve recovery from acute illness."[46] Again,

> At a meeting of the American College of Cardiology . . . Duke researcher Dr. Mitchell Krucoff reported preliminary data on a national trial of 750 patients undergoing heart catheterization or angioplasty. A group of patients who were prayed for (by, among others, Roman Catholics and Sufi Muslims in the United States, Buddhist monks in Nepal and Jews at the Western Wall) did no better than a second group that received standard care or a third, which was given a special program of music, therapeutic touch and guided imagery . . . . Overall, the prayer studies have not shown clear effects . . . . [47]

Most important, however, in 2006 the results were released of "the most scientifically rigorous investigation of whether prayer can heal illness," a study that lasted almost ten years and involved more than 1,800 patients. The conclusion: "Prayers offered by strangers had no effect on the recovery of people who were undergoing heart surgery. . . ."[48]

If convincing positive evidence of prayer's power seems to be lacking, there is concern among some scientists that religious faith might actually *interfere with* health. "In her review of the literature,

[Lynda] Powell found several studies suggesting that praying with a sick person can sometimes impede recovery; one study concluded that the risk of bad health outcome doubled, perhaps because patients believed God would protect them or that their illness was some kind of divine punishment."[49]

While there can be little doubt that the healthy lifestyle—lack of drug abuse, for example—and the generally optimistic attitude that often accompany religious practice can have positive health benefits, and while it is certainly good medical practice for physicians to be sensitive to their patients' spiritual attitudes, the empirical evidence for divine action in response to prayer in matters of health is nil. It seems that everywhere we turn, we encounter evidence that science and traditional religious belief do not cohere after all.

This all-too-brief survey of the contemporary discussion of God's influence upon the world cannot do justice to the complex issues involved. But it does at least point to the vast difficulties that the present-day scientific worldview poses for biblical theism. The conviction that God can act within creation, and especially within the lives of human beings, is surely crucial to the whole tradition of biblical theism. Yet, for the three-quarters of a century that contemporary physics has been with us, theologians have been unable to construct any scientifically plausible account of how such divine action is possible. Their recent efforts have been more concerted, but no more successful than what was attempted in decades past. It would be hard to overestimate the significance of this apparent failure, given the centrality of the scientific worldview today for cultures around the globe.

The Inescapability of the Confrontation between Science and Theology

I have argued that the results of the current dialogue between traditional theism and contemporary science are, thus far, a failure, particularly regarding God's action in the world. But there are many Christian theologians, perhaps even a majority of them, who will react to my conclusion with yawns rather than with cries of dismay. While there have always been Christians who believe that scientific and religious claims intersect and sometimes conflict—peace will reign only if one side vanquishes the other or if they can be brought into harmony with one another—many other Christian thinkers hold that religion and science occupy wholly separate spheres. For this latter camp, neither conflict nor coalescence is an applicable category in talking about the relationship between science and faith. As already indicated, John Henry Newman, for example, saw no need to oppose Darwin's teachings on evolution, in sharp contrast to the familiar fundamentalist attacks on Darwinism, from the Scopes trial to "creationism."[50] For Newman, religion and science each have separate tasks, and there is no need for them to do battle.[51]

The Separatist Stance

It seems only natural for theologians of a traditional bent to maintain that God, indeed, does act, and does act continuously, within the natural sphere, but that such action is visible only to the eyes of faith. Science deals with the empirically observable; faith and theology, with the transcendent. The transcendent can definitely impinge upon the world of nature, but in a fashion necessarily invisible to the instruments of scientific inquiry (and even faith, while it can see the results of this impingement, cannot explain how it works). Science and faith speak wholly separate languages. This separatist stance apparently makes sense not only to theologians who are happily ensconced within the Christian tradition, but also to those who are susceptible to intellectual claustrophobia and wish to operate "on the boundary" between the Christian tradition and contemporary society. The notion that theology should be done on the boundaries is particularly associated with Paul Tillich and his heirs. Yet, when it comes to the relationship between religion and science, Tillich unequivocally embraces the separatist stance, at least if his *Dynamics of Faith* is a reliable guide: "Scientific truth and the truth of faith do not belong to the same dimension of meaning. Science has no right and no power to interfere with faith and faith has no power to interfere with science. One dimension of meaning is not able to interfere with another dimension."[52]

Tillich's succinct formulation is a useful guide to the separatist position, especially insofar as it clearly expresses the practical benefits of thinking of science and faith as wholly independent of one another. A great deal of unpleasantness can be avoided by agreeing to the separatist approach. Theologians who endorse the separatist pact need not worry about scientific discoveries eroding the Christian worldview, and scientists can embrace that same pact as a restraining order against crusading fundamentalists. It is unsurprising, then, that many scientists find the separatist tack as enticing as their theological counterparts do. It is a tack taken, for instance, in the late Stephen Jay Gould's book on the relationship between religion and science, *Rocks of Ages*. The heart of Gould's proposal is that both religious persons and scientists should abide by the notion that he dubs "NOMA," for "Non-Overlapping Magisteria." Religion has its arena of teaching authority, and science, its arena, and the two do not overlap. Religion is about "human purposes, meanings, and values," while to science must be left questions about the origin and behavior of the natural world.[53] While science and religion can have some interesting insights to pass along to one another, they are up to entirely separate tasks, a position that Gould finds (rightly, I believe) in Pope John Paul II's pronouncements on evolution and that has produced "a strong consensus accepted for decades by leading scientific and religious thinkers alike."[54]

Gould has no time, then, for any attempts at what he calls "syncretism," the effort to meld science and religion into some larger harmonious position. Indeed, he confesses, with undisguised irritation, "I find the arguments of syncretism so flawed, so illogical, so based in hope alone, and so freighted by past procedures and certainties, that I have difficulty keeping a straight face or a peaceful pen."[55] He goes on to explain, "I feel particularly sensitive about this issue because, as I wrote this book in the summer of 1998, a deluge of media hype enveloped the syncretist position, as though some startlingly new and persuasive argument had been formulated, or some equally exciting and transforming discovery had been made. In fact, absolutely nothing of intellectual novelty had been added . . . ."[56]

It is quite obvious, then, that for those theologians and scientists committed to the separatist route, the attempts of theologians such as Peacocke, Polkinghorne, and Murphy to harmonize science and faith seem naive and misguided. That attempt at harmony assumes that theological claims, if not carefully crafted, can *violate* the tenets of natural science. But if, as the separatist party maintains, science and religion operate in wholly different realms of meaning, or are akin to different languages, then the notion of violation could not possibly apply here. Suppose that I grow up in a bilingual household so that I am fluent in both Spanish and English. When I choose to speak Spanish, there is no relevant sense in which I am violating the rules of English. Speaking in Spanish is a distinct enterprise from speaking English, while complaining "I can't get no satisfaction" is a violation of the rules of English grammar, however felicitous.

Problems with the Separatist Stance

The fundamental difficulty here, however, is that science and religion are simply not entirely incommensurable arenas, and comparing science and religion to two different languages is misleading. At least, they are not entirely separate if we include under the heading of religion the belief in a personal God who self-consciously acts within the world of nature that God has created. Suppose that instead of thinking of science and religious as separate languages, we apply the alternative metaphor of different "circles of meaning." There can be no doubt that religion and science are circles of meaning with quite different center points. But distinct circles can still intersect to varying degrees. And, in fact, the admittedly distinct circles of science and faith do intersect when it comes to something such as talk of divine action in the world. While God's hand may be visible only to the eyes of faith, it is nonetheless true that, in many cases, the effects of that alleged divine activity must be public property. In other words, that it was *God* who effected a particular action is visible only from the perspective of faith; *what* was effected will be open to scientific scrutiny.[57] There are innumerable concrete cases that could be used to illustrate this fact. Some of those cases are more helpful than others, however. That some Christians still pray to God for rain, for instance, makes many within the contemporary Christian community uncomfortable. Hence, let us consider a case that is, arguably, plausible for the vast majority of present-day Christians.

Suppose that, when I am in a state of despair, I pray to God and then find my mindset transformed. Desperation is replaced by optimism and torpor by renewed vigor. The separatist will most likely describe what happens in this case by saying that God has acted to give me strength, but that only the eyes of faith can see that it was, in fact, the work of God. Science will find nothing unusual in this transformation because science by its very nature is confined to a dimension of reality wholly separate from the transcendent reality of God and God's action. Here is the confusion, though: as indicated above, while one may claim that only faith is privy to the fact that it was God who acted, the result of that action is publicly observable, at least in principle, even when we are talking about something as apparently private as a change in my mental state. For my mood to change, my brain chemistry much change: dopamine will flow, serotonin levels will rise, electrical activity will increase—whatever the details, the change will, in principle, be more than evident to scientific scrutiny. And any such change will entail expenditure of energy. If this energy is introduced by God (however far back in some perhaps exceedingly long causal chain)—if it is not simply part of a series of events that was going to occur in any case, with or without God—the conservation law is violated. In short, the stance according to which science and religion are wholly separate realms does not succeed in removing all elements of a theological claim from scientific investigation. As neurologist Andrew Newberg puts it, "Neurology makes it clear: There's no other way for God to get into your head except through the brain's neural pathways."[58] The crucial fact of the matter is that the elements of the claim of divine action that are left in plain view, the alleged effects of that action, are sufficient for the scientist to detect a violation of the conservation of energy.

The Unavoidable Challenge

Suppose that we return at this point to Stephen Jay Gould's defense of the separatist position. That defense gives every sign of being heartfelt, and it is unquestionably eloquent. How is it, then, that Gould fails to see that the separatist stance cannot be maintained, that claims of God's action in the world necessarily impinge upon the principles of science? The answer is not difficult to find: Gould works with an extraordinarily attenuated notion of religion according to which the religious person will not make such claims of divine action in the world. Looking to the etymology of the term *religion*, Gould counts "as fundamentally religious (literally, binding us together) all moral discourse on principles that might activate the ideal of universal fellowship among people."[59] While this approach assigns some extraordinarily lofty issues to the magisterium of religion, any reference to the ability of God to act within the natural world is conspicuously absent. Indeed, Gould seems to suppose that all but fundamentalists will take it for granted that it simply makes no sense to talk about God accomplishing something within the natural world that is in addition to what the world does on its own. And when he turns to evolution, Gould holds that the science of evolution dictates that the rise of the human species was purely a matter of chance; there is no point in trying to make the origin of *Homo Sapiens* consistent with a special divine intention to have human beings appear on the scene.[60] Gould's defense of the separatist stance, then, offers little solace to what is, in fact, the view of the vast majority of Christian thinkers.

It should be clear from the foregoing that the Christian theist faces a significant challenge. The issue is not simply that science is unable to understand how God acts. Rather, the issue is that assertions about God's work in the world appear actually to violate basic scientific principles. And to say that religious convictions violate scientific principles is a very different matter from saying that faith and science speak different languages. Violating the tenets of the scientific worldview when operating religiously is not akin to speaking English some of the time and Spanish the rest of the time, nor is it like writing poetry on Monday and working out mathematical equations on Tuesday. Rather, it is akin to failing at speaking a particular language, or to coming up with the wrong answers to mathematical problems. The vast majority of Christians in North America and the rest of the so-called "first world" embrace the bulk of the scientific worldview as an accurate description of physical reality. While they may be uncertain about what science has to say about evolution, today's Christians have imbibed the scientific worldview on everything from germs to black holes. They should be no more sanguine—indeed, they should be decidedly less sanguine—about violating scientific principles than they would be about speaking ungrammatically or making mathematical errors. That is why what Peacocke, Polkinghorne, and Murphy are attempting is not naive, but, rather, crucial for the integrity of Christian faith, at least as they conceive Christian belief.

Recall that their enterprise, modestly conceived, does not necessitate coming up with a definitive explanation of how God does, in fact, operate within the physical world. It simply entails showing a way, or ways, of understanding how God *could* accomplish what Christian faith says God accomplishes within the world, without violating principles such as the conservation of energy. Unfortunately, at least as far as I can tell, Murphy and her colleagues, brilliant though they be, have not yet succeeded in even this modest task.

For much of the modern period, Christian faith never seriously grappled with the worldview erected by natural science. Fundamentalists supposed that they could get away with declaring that scientific precepts were simply false whenever they seemed to contradict biblical faith, a misapprehension under which their creationist offspring sometimes still apparently labor. More sophisticated believers, and especially the professional theologians among them, were apt to argue that religion and science do not overlap and, hence, cannot get in each other's way. Nor, for a good portion of the modern period, were theologians even given the opportunity to confront what we now regard as the scientific worldview: quantum physics, along with our fundamental perceptions about cosmology, did not come along until the twentieth century and is, of course, still developing.

It is no longer possible, however, for Christian thinkers to avoid science. The basic outlines of the scientific worldview have become part of the background beliefs of the vast majority of first world persons. Today, anyone who declares that the scientific perspective is fundamentally in error in its description of the physical universe only succeeds in removing himself or herself from serious participation in the conversation. The separatist stance, while it attempts to respect science's claims to understanding, is quickly losing its inertia as we confront the particulars of both theological and scientific claims. Those scientifically erudite theologians who have attempted to harmonize God's action in the world with science are to be congratulated for their efforts. But thus far, their efforts have all run aground. It is no accident that a survey of members of the prestigious National Academy of Sciences reported that only *7 percent* believe in a personal God![61]

The Dawkins Dilemma

This reference to contemporary practitioners of the natural sciences bookends our discussion by bringing us back to Richard Dawkins's *The God Delusion*. Dawkins actually attempts to do more in that book than merely to show the incompatibility of theism and science: he adduces what he takes to be scientific evidence that comes close to ruling out the possibility of God's existence.[62] For Dawkins, what science has learned about evolution means that there "almost certainly" is no God. Science has determined that more complex beings evolve, over a long period of time, out of simpler ones. How, then, should we conceive the First Cause of the universe if there be such a thing? Theists after Aristotle have claimed that God is the First Cause.[63] But, says Dawkins, that would be to put the most complex reality imaginable, namely God, at the *beginning* of time, which is exactly where it could not be if the rule holds that complexity comes at the *end* of a long process of development.

It must be said that Dawkins is putting an awful lot of argumentative eggs in this one basket. Might not God, by God's very nature, be an exception to a rule that has arisen from our knowledge of physical beings? Marilynne Robinson trots out the traditional theological claim, for example, that God stands outside of time and is, therefore, not subject to the principles of the evolution of complex organisms, whose principles are necessarily temporal.[64] Of course, merely to say that God stands outside time and to leave it at that, as Robinson does, is to evoke a spatial metaphor with precious little conceptual oomph. The point, in any case, is that well-known scientists can now be enlisted to bolster the contention that science and religion cannot as easily be harmonized as some religious thinkers would have us believe.

The popular press is notoriously fickle and is always attuned to which way the wind is blowing. It should probably not be surprising, then, that the sort of cover stories about the convergence of science and religion that were cited above, at the outset of our discussion, seem suddenly to be out of fashion. The October 13, 2006, cover of *Time* magazine bore the words "God vs. Science." Michael Brooks, writing in *New Scientist* addressed the issue, "In Place of God: Can Secular Science Ever Oust Religious Belief—and Should It Even Try?"[65] And Gary Wolf penned an article for the November 2006 issue of *Wired,* titled "The New Atheism: No Heaven. No Hell. Just Science. Inside the Crusade against Religion."[66]

However one chooses to react to the pronouncements of the popular media, we do face an unprecedented moment in the history of Christian theism. Could it be that Christian thought will, finally, prove unable to deal with the regnant intellectual achievement of our culture? The scientific worldview is not about to undergo truly fundamental changes anytime soon. Thus, one can plausibly argue that if religion is to be productively harmonized with science, we must look to a form of religion and theology different from traditional Christian theism. Might it be that we would have better luck linking *radical* theologies with science? I believe that we most definitely would. Yet, it is not difficult to imagine how some scientific opponents of traditional theism will react to a theologically radical approach to science: "Why bother?" In other words, if we abandon the God of traditional theism—the God who can answer prayer, guide history, and provide eternal life—aren't we left with a God too ineffectual to worry about? This is probably the preeminent challenge to be faced by the claim that radical theology shows the way to coherence between spirituality and science. It is a challenge that will, in effect, be at issue throughout the pages that follow.

CHAPTER TWO

Radical Theology: Uniting Science and Religion

As already indicated, radical theology is a position that rejects the notion of a transcendent personal consciousness who created the universe; it finds the ultimate in some alternative dimension of reality. In chapter three, we will zero in on a particular brand of radical theology, one that champions pantheism. But such a notion of the divine may seem a nonstarter when it comes to harmonizing religion and science. The present chapter attempts to defuse the claim that radical theology is inimical to science.

Radical theology as a genre may appear to have characteristics that make it resistant, if not simply antithetical, to the scientific world picture. Four issues in particular will be considered here: first, possible contagion from New Age spirituality; second, the claim frequently associated with postmodernism—a mindset sometimes linked with radical theology—that science is simply one language game among others, with no special insight into the reality of nature; third, the notion sometimes held by radical eco-theologies that science is a cold and manipulative device that denudes rather than nurtures the earth and its inhabitants; and fourth, the possibility that any harmony achieved between a radical theology and science will result from the complete capitulation of the theologian's concept of deity to the scientific worldview so that the concept of deity will be evacuated of significant content.

Radical Theology and the New Age

As we shall see in chapter three, one of the most important radical theologians of the present moment is Mary Daly. Her work is radical both in its thoroughgoing, insistent feminism and in its re-conceptualization of the divine. Daly's God is no longer the transcendent Father of her Roman Catholic upbringing, but an immanent power of being that fructifies the universe and in which women can immediately participate. Such a deity is, by its very nature, not merely an object for abstract intellectual investigation, but an empowering force to which one should open oneself. But how does one do this if not through newly minted, sometimes idiosyncratic spiritual disciplines and rituals? And once that be said, can New Age spirituality be far behind? In other words, it may frequently appear as if the practical application of radical notions of divinity necessarily places one in the New Age camp. A glance at actual feminist spirituality, after all, reveals practices such as healing the body through balancing its chakras (seven "energy centers"), telling the future via astrology, and manipulating reality through magic.[1] None of these practices is out of step with what is usually called New Age spirituality, but they could scarcely be more alien to the scientific perspective.

The New Age camp, then, is hardly the place where one wants to be seen if she wishes to claim harmony with the natural sciences. A September 2003 search of the Barnesandnoble.com website, using the keyword string "New Age spirituality," produced 563 titles, many of which might make the scientifically inclined wish that we could send New Age authors off to other planets (where, by the way, many of them would clearly be quite at home). There is *Saint Germain's Prophecy for the New Millenium: Includes Dramatic Prophecies from Nostradamus, Edgar Cayce, and Mother Mary* (rather strange bedfellows, one would think).[2] Or, if you wish to be your own seer, you can read *The Complete Idiot's Guide to Tarot and Fortune-Telling*.[3] Of course, astrology is ever present, as in *Astrology and Consciousness: The Wheel of Light*.[4] Then there is *Archangels and Ascended Masters: A Guide to Working and Healing with Divinities and Deities*.[5] On the topic of the auras that we supposedly cast, one can read Edgar Cayce's *Auras: An Essay on the Meaning of Colors*.[6] Or perhaps *Shamanic Experience: A Practical Guide to Psychic Powers,* which the publisher's note claims can help you "develop relationships with power animals, discover your aura, and energize your power centers."[7] Who would want to miss *The Complete Ascension Manual for the Aquarian Age: How to Achieve Ascension in This Lifetime,* which the publisher explains is "compiled from research and channeled information"?[8] "Channeling" is the notion of becoming a conduit for communications from the dead. Finally, one might choose to place on one's bedside table *Dream Book: Dream Spells, Nighttime Potions and Rituals, and Other Magical Sleep Formulas.*[9]

If this is where radical theology ends up, practically speaking, then radical theologians can give up any hope of a fruitful dialogue with the natural sciences. Not surprisingly, my claim is that there is no *necessary* connection between sophisticated radical theologies and New Age spiritual practice. After all, consider the case of orthodox Christian belief and practice. The traditional Christian is buttressed by centuries of elegant theological reflection, from Augustine to Thomas Aquinas to Karl Barth and beyond. Furthermore, he or she has venerable and precise creeds behind him, such as the Apostle' Creed and the Nicene Creed. Yet, this does not stop the occasional orthodox Christian from seeing the reflection of Jesus in a fishbowl, nor does it prevent him, in a difficult real estate market, from burying the statue of a saint on his property so that his house might sell more quickly. In other words, all religious traditions contain both serious reflection and frivolous, superstitious practices. Yet, that does not mean that there is any necessity of moving from the one to the other: the majority of orthodox Christians find little spiritual illumination in their fishbowls and are only infrequently seen burying statues in their yards. Hence, while there might appear to be some natural affinities between radical theologies and New Age spirituality—the freedom to throw off tradition and move into new spiritual territory on one's own initiative plays a part in both, for example—both radical theology and the practice to which it leads can steer clear of New Age mumbo jumbo. Indeed, radical theologian Mary Daly, with whose work we began this reflection, dismisses in no uncertain terms the "massively passivizing effects of the therapeutic establishment or of 'New Age' style 'Goddess' spirituality."[10] Daly makes this dismissal despite the fact that she is quite willing to use Goddess symbolism herself, as when she draws upon the image of the ancient Egyptian goddess Isis. But she wants to make sure that, in contrast to New Age usage, her own Goddess symbolism is not privatizing and, as she says, "passivizing," in other words, that it does not draw one into an isolated, self-absorbed piety. And she sees to it that her references to the Goddess are firmly grounded in her own sophisticated theological (or "thealogical," from the Greek word for goddess) reflections. On the positive side, then, radical theology can move beyond the tenets of classical theism without embracing the inanities of much New Age spirituality.

Radical Theology and the Postmodern

We can now move onto the second challenge facing radical theology in its efforts to connect with science. An important sub-genre of radical theology during the last part of the twentieth century and on into the twenty-first has been what can loosely be called *postmodern* theology. We are concerned here not with conservative appropriations of the concept of the postmodern—George Lindbeck's notion of "post-liberal" theology, for example—but of so-called left-wing postmodernism. The philosophical leaders in this movement include theorists such as Jacques Derrida, Julia Kristeva, Jean Baudrillard, and Jean François Lyotard. Among those who have appropriated postmodern theory for radical theological purposes are Mark C. Taylor, Edith Wyschogrod, and Charles Winquist.[11]

In his influential manifesto, *The Postmodern Condition*, Lyotard provides us a handy characterization of the postmodern mindset. Postmodernism, he says, is characterized by "incredulity toward metanarratives."[12] That is, the postmodernist rejects the idea that there is some super-narrative, some one overarching story that contains all other stories within itself. Rather, we confront separate language games, each with its own internal rules for what constitutes valid knowing. Doctrinaire Marxism is (or was) a metanarrative. Religions such as Judaism, Christianity, and Islam offer metanarratives: each purports to tell the whole story of the world and the human project, from creation to divine consummation, and every other sort of human story can purportedly be fit under the umbrella of this religious metanarrative. But in the postmodern era, says Lyotard, all claims to knowledge face a crisis of legitimation. We no longer take for granted theistic religion's appeals to revelation, for example, nor science's claim to have indubitable access to nature via a perfectly objective and universal, value-free empirical method. What happens to natural science, then? It becomes just another language game for describing the world, its operating principles applying only internally, that is, to the game itself, as is true with all language games. The language game of science has the peculiar characteristic of intentionally being internally destabilizing: the role of the scientific theorist is to propose ever-new ideas, which will bring something different to the scientific game and challenge its players to react.

A component that is especially important in this Lyotardian view, one that other postmodernists frequently share (the conservative, such as Lindbeck, as well as the radical), is that there is no meta-position from which it is possible to compare language games and their relation to nature and to show that science has a uniquely realistic grasp of the natural world. We are, in essence, back to Nietzsche: science is a useful fiction. We will regard it as "true" not in some constant and objective sense, but just in those circumstances where it is useful in accomplishing a goal that answers to what Nietzsche would, of course, identify as our will to power. Now, if radical theology adopts this view, it is going to have a great deal of trouble in being taken seriously by contemporary scientists, because practicing scientists seldom if ever adopt the radical postmodern perspective on their trade. Rather, for the scientific community, science has a uniquely realistic perspective on the world, and science makes genuine, measurable progress in adding to the storehouse of knowledge.[13]

As I have suggested, however, Lyotard is by no means alone among postmodernist theorists in offering a view of science that radically undermines the scientific community's self-understanding. A case in point is the philosopher of science Paul Feyerabend. Although he is inconsistent in his pronouncements, in his more incautious moments, Feyerabend can assert, for example, that science is a "particular superstition."[14] As it turns out, however, postmodern commentators on science may be their own worst enemies. If one is going to argue for a radically new interpretation of what scientists are up to, he had best at least understand the particular mathematical and scientific perspectives at issue. But such understanding, it turns out, is only rarely in evidence. To take but two examples, scientists Alan Sokal and Alan Bricmont point out that Julia Kristeva gets Gödel's famous theorem (which has to do with the impossibility of proving within a mathematical system the consistency of that system) exactly backwards.[15] Other provocative postmodernists such as Jean Baudrillard fare no better.

It cannot be denied that some radical theologians have essentially bought into the postmodernist attitude toward science represented by Lyotard and his compatriots. An apparent case in point is a book that is often regarded as the founding and single most important work in the genre of radical postmodernist theology, Mark C. Taylor's *Erring: A Postmodern A/Theology*. First of all, it is highly significant that Taylor barely mentions science. In a grandiose undertaking that surveys the topics of God, self, history, and the book, science is scarcely worth referencing. When Taylor does mention it, he tells us that

> Early scientific investigators argued that all of nature is potentially "for us." In order to realize this potential, the searching scientist had to put nature "to the rack and compel her [*sic*] to answer our questions." From this point of view, the world is intended to respond to human probing and to serve *man's* purposes.[16]

This reading of science is not necessarily postmodernist just in and of itself (indeed, it will be central to our third topic, investigated below), but it fits well into that postmodernist perspective that rejects the traditional scientific claim to objective, "truth"-yielding access to the really real.

How can one defend radical theology's potential to work productively with science when postmodern theory so often rejects the scientific enterprise as it is understood by scientists themselves? First of all, postmodernist radical theology is only one sub-genre of the larger undertaking that is radical theology. Radical theology as such, in other words, is not beholden to the left-wing postmodernists' misperceptions of science. Second, as Sokal and Bricmont show, the most outspoken postmodern critics of science—we have mentioned Lyotard, Kristeva, and Baudrillard, for example—have disqualified themselves as commentators upon science, simply via their appalling ignorance of what science even claims to be saying. On the other hand, as I indicated in chapter one, I do not equate radical theology with an embrace of the naïve foundationalist claims about science sometimes set forth in the Enlightenment.

Ecotheology and Radical Theology

We encounter another sort of suspicion about science, if a more nuanced one, in the work of Rosemary Radford Ruether. She is sometimes classified as a "reforming" theologian rather than as a "radical" one. But this assessment has to do with the specific arguments among women within the Christian tradition: "conservatives" hold that all is as it should be—women need not be ordained priests, and the divine need not be de-masculinized, for example—while "reformers" hold that the Christian tradition needs to be reformed via feminist sensibilities, and the "radicals" assert that Christianity is so systemically patriarchal so that women have no choice but to abandon it and return to ancient goddess spiritualities or variations thereupon. But, however one wishes to classify Ruether's feminism, her view of the divine is surely radically different from what is provided by orthodox Christianity. Her God/ess is not a supernatural personal consciousness who stands beyond the world it created, but rather the "Primal Matrix" ("matrix" is from the Latin for womb, and indirectly, from mother) that embraces all within it. Does this God/ess whisk us off to heaven after we die? Not necessarily, for death and change are good, and death follows from our finitiude; only God/ess is infinite.[17]

One of the implications that Ruether draws from her notion of the Primal Matrix is that we ought to overcome the traditional dualism of spirit vs. matter: the latter is just as sacred as the former. Her theological ecology comes to full expression in *Gaia and God: An Ecofeminist Theology of Earth Healing*.[18] As Ruether explains,

"*Gaia* is the word for the Greek Earth Goddess, and it is also a term adopted by a group of planetary biologists, such as James Lovelock and Lynn Margulis, to refer to their thesis that the entire planet is a living system, behaving as a unified organism."[19] Science obviously has a role in the sort of earth healing Ruether seeks. After all, it is the science of ecology that gives us the insight we genuinely need to heal the earth. Indeed, ecology is a branch of science that dovetails with ethics:

> Ecology is the biological science of biotic communities that demonstrates the laws by which nature, unaided by humans, has generated and sustained life. In addition, its study also suggests guidelines for how humans must learn to live as a sustaining, rather than destructive, member of such biotic communities. Thus, unlike those modern physical and biological sciences that have claimed to be only descriptive, ecology suggests some restoration of the classical role of science as normative or as ethically prescriptive.[20]

However, while ecology is close to Ruether's heart, she is much more suspicious about natural science in general. It has not, in fact, been value-free, she tells us. It is not purely objective, as it claims, but is often subjective. Worst of all, science produces technologies that may well destroy the earth rather than save it.[21] The scientific method itself, especially as inherited from Francis Bacon, is essentially destructive from the outset. Bacon thinks in terms of witch-hunting: the laboratory is the Inquisitor's chamber in which the scientist will torture nature until she is forced to give up her secrets. "Bacon's thought is pervaded by images of nature as a female to be coerced, 'penetrated,' conquered and forced to 'yield,' the language of rape and subjugation of women, while the scientist is imaged as the epitome of masculine power. . . ."[22]

For all that, Ruether is not deaf to the call of the "common creation story" that Sallie McFague attributes to contemporary science (on which more will be addressed below).[23] Muses Ruether, "If the new cosmic stories of astral and atomic physics and ecology are to provide a new and shared planetary 'myth' for ethics and spirituality, as well as scientific understanding, it is necessary to heal the splits between 'fact' and 'value,' theory and practice, private and social, that have been created in Western thought."[24] It will be part of the burden of proof borne by the chapters that follow to show that, far from being a tool for destructively dissecting nature, the scientific worldview can indeed serve as an ecologically sensitive and spiritually energizing planetary myth.

The word *myth* is being used here in the technical sense employed in disciplines such as religious studies. It refers not to primitive explanations of the world nor to mere "tall tales," but suggests a narrative with powerful symbolic dimensions. The common creation story provided by science is, taken just in and of itself, a literal account of the cosmos and its evolution, not a symbolic story. But the spiritual quester can easily apply that literal account to her quest in a way that gives the story symbolic value, in other words, that points beyond the story's literal account of the world to its existential implications for human life. Radical theology's evaluation of the scientific worldview will then be a decidedly positive one.

Is Radical Theology a Capitulation?

Finally, a fourth problem initially confronting the notion of placing science and radical theology in fruitful dialogue involves this question: is radical theology's consistency with science finally empty, with a consistency resulting from the fact that radical theology has simply pruned from its concept of God any attributes that could contradict scientific claims? Let us divide our discussion of this issue into two tasks. First, we must distinguish the potential problem at hand from the so-called "separatist" stance on science and religion that we discussed in chapter one. Traditional Christian theism holds to a God who is a transcendent personal consciousness who created the world and who acts within it. This God is omnipotent and omniscient. Yet, maintain the separatists, claims about this God's actions within the world and human life need not conflict with science because scientific claims and religious claims occupy wholly separate realms. But we saw that the separatists were simply mistaken in thinking that they could, in fact, keep science and their theistic stance separate: their God's actions in the world are not simply supernatural events visible only to the eyes of faith and somehow hidden from the purview of science. On the contrary, the alleged divine activity will always run afoul of basic scientific principles, such as the law of the conservation of mass and energy.

Some might initially suppose that to say that radical theology purchases consistency with science at the price of abandoning any claims that would conflict with science, is essentially to hold that radical theology embraces the separatist strategy. But we have seen that the separatist does not really abandon any of her claims about God and God's power to act in the world; she wants to have her cake and eat it too. Hence, the separatist position breaks down when it is carefully investigated.

By contrast, the radical theologies that we shall consider will, at least for the most part, be consistent with science because they actually do deny any power to the divine that would interfere with the scientific worldview. The problem that must subsequently be faced, then, is whether radical theology gives up too much. Is the price of compliance with science's dictates an impotent deity to whom the proper response is mere indifference? Here the proof, one can only say, must be in the pudding. Let us see, in other words, what radical theologians are able to do with their deities. Are they able to make those deities fundamental sources of meaning and guidance for human life? Are they able to find poetry and power there? And will the Gods and Goddesses of radical theology be able to appropriate the scientific worldview creatively and in such a way that this worldview becomes a crucial component of our spiritual attunement to the world? I wager that we shall be able to answer each of these questions in the affirmative.

My optimism is based upon a number of considerations about radical theology. Let us briefly consider five. First, radical theologians tend to emphasize divine immanence. Rather than thinking of God as the *pantocrator*, a heavenly king who sits on a throne high above his creation, deity is understood as permeating the world of nature. Far from being mere "stuff" that comes off second-best when compared to "spirit," the material world is itself a part of the Godhead and hence worthy of the deepest reverence. This characteristic of radical theology certainly predisposes it to be sympathetic and attentive to the realities that science explores.

Second, radical theologies tend to put a special investment in reason in their pursuit of a satisfying spirituality. Christian theology has always involved some dialogue between faith and reason, but reason has often come off second-best. Held on a short leash, reason is ultimately controlled by authority and tradition, or it is simply abandoned as one engages in a blind leap of faith. But radical theology, by its very nature, throws off subservience to authority and tradition, and it is powered by unfettered exploration of the world and humanity's place within it. We shall see, for example, that the theologies of Sallie McFague, Gordon Kaufman, and Ursula Goodenough are highly rational, though their rationality is not cold and isolating, but always in the service of a fruitful spirituality. This commitment to unfettered reason on the part of radical theology is a second characteristic that renders it an appropriate dialogue partner with science.

Of course, there is once again the potentially troubling matter of the postmodernist sub-genre of radical theology. The relation of postmodernist theory to reason, and also to science, is ambiguous. On the one hand, to read the work of Jacques Derrida, for instance, is to encounter a mind that can dazzle by its brilliance. On the other hand, much postmodernist writing—Derrida's should sometimes be included here—is full of mind-boggling neologisms that essentially constitute a private language. Such writing is indicative of what can only be called a pseudo-rationality. It may be true that if one wishes to deconstruct ordinary discourse and knowledges, it is necessary to fashion tools that are in some sense foreign to such discourse and knowledges. Nonetheless, one who ends up with a private language cannot, by definition, open his or her thinking up to the larger human community. And it then follows that one's own postmodernist discourse is not rational, for a hallmark of rationality is the willingness to submit one's beliefs and attitudes to the scrutiny of others (or, as postmodernists themselves might say, to the scrutiny of "the other"). Postmodernist theory is caught in an understandable bind, then, but it is a bind that most other forms of radical theology avoid.

Third, while the English word *radical* goes back to the Latin word for "root," radical theology as I am using the phrase is hardly interested in going back to some ancient worldview that provides the roots of orthodox Christianity. Rather, it is radical in the sense of breaking the bonds of the past and ever pushing ahead into new and unexplored territory. Radical theology has an affinity for the contemporary, which will also draw it naturally into conversation with science.

Fourth, radical theologies frequently have a universalistic bent. They are willing to draw upon a diversity of spiritual traditions and resources, from Hinduism, Buddhism, and Taoism to preliterate goddess traditions. But what provides the glue among different cultures and perspectives in the present day and age? What is our *lingua franca*? Surely, it is the scientific worldview, what Sallie McFague quite rightly calls the "common creation story." The common creation story is the one that begins with the Big Bang and moves through events such as nucleo-synthesis in stars, the appearance of life on earth, and the evolutionary struggle that has produced *Homo Sapiens* as one of its many offspring. Thus, a universalistic bent is one more factor inclining radical theology to a dialogue with science, since science is contemporary culture's universal language.

Fifth, radical theology is by its very nature more humanistic than traditional theologies. Radical theologies, as already noted, emphasize divine immanence. What this means in practical human terms is that the human itself, along with its natural environment, necessarily participates in sacrality. Deity is limited and works alongside humanity and nature rather than omnipotently manipulating it from afar. Radical theology's emphasis upon the human—an emphasis that only rarely goes so far as to naively deify humanity—an emphasis upon the natural (human beings in their environment) rather than the supernatural, is but one more characteristic that puts it on the same wavelength upon which science broadcasts.

CHAPTER THREE

Beyond Theism: A Scientifically Informed Pantheism

In this chapter, we shall look at four radical theologians—Sallie McFague, Mary Daly, Gordon Kaufman, and Ursula Goodenough (Goodenough normally wears a cell biologist's hat, but dons theological garb from time to time too)—and explore how their thought coheres with the contemporary scientific worldview. It will not be my claim that each of their theologies, just as it is, fits perfectly with contemporary science; rather, I shall suggest that there are numerous elements in each of their approaches that make each a rich resource for serious dialogue with the scientific worldview. But what is more, I shall argue that by pushing the first three thinkers to be just a bit more radical than they already are, they can, in fact, provide science-friendly theologies more consistently. We shall see that Ursula Goodenough's theology is already in attire sufficiently radical that it does not need any refinements. Once our brief survey is complete, I shall outline a contemporary, scientifically informed pantheism and augment it with insights from the four thinkers in the survey.

Sallie McFague's Empowering Spirit

We begin with the work of Sallie McFague.[1] We have already mentioned McFague's insightful notion of the "common creation story," by which she means, essentially, the Big Bang cosmology, the formation of stars and planets, and the Darwinian account of biological evolution. This story is, indeed, embraced by a vast number of educated persons around the world in diverse cultures. Now McFague does not initially appear as terribly radical. She considers herself a Christian theologian, one who supposes that there is a personal and benevolent power behind the universe and that this power is potently revealed in the figure of Jesus of Nazareth.[2] In other ways, however, McFague does, in fact, embrace a radical perspective. She considers herself "feminist, skeptical, relativistic," and also "iconoclastic," and she cannot embrace "an incarnational christology or a canonical Scripture."[3] Indeed, she goes so far as to proclaim that we can actually know very little about the Christian faith and that "Theology is mostly fiction."[4] This modest approach to our knowledge of the divine leads McFague to her hallmark emphasis on the role of metaphors and models in theology. A metaphor attempts to say a bit about what something "is," but at the same time it contains an important "is not." In Shakespeare's double metaphor from *Macbeth*, "sleep that knits up the raveled sleeve of care," we know that sleep is in some ways like a knitter, and care, in some ways like a raveled sleeve, but, of course, they are not literally so: there is a large element of the "is not" in metaphor.

Due to our paucity of knowledge about the divine, we must employ the modest device that is metaphor, with its powerful "is not." A model is an extension of metaphor that includes a larger conceptual element, a metaphor that can be a powerful tool for leading us into reflection. Scientists are, of course, quite familiar with models and their usefulness. For instance, to take a very simple example, they might visualize Einstein's description of gravitation in four-dimensional space-time in his General Theory of Relativity in terms of a two-dimensional rubber sheet on which a steel ball (representing our sun) creates a large depression that will cause a lighter marble, standing for the Earth, to be pulled toward it. But to say that theology is "mostly fiction" and that it must employ metaphors and models is not to say that it is *entirely* imaginative, a mere flight of fancy. On the contrary, McFague adopts a form of *pragmatism* according to which a true account of God and God's relation to the world is one that articulates the most useful approach to Christian faith for our own time and situation.[5] That particular account of Christian faith is true because it does not simply pass on traditional creeds and sensibilities, but because it allows the spirit of Christianity to inform our own cultural and existential situation. And lest scientists consider this still a suspiciously postmodern attitude, an insufficiently robust epistemology, McFague openly aligns herself with what philosophers of science call "critical or modified realism."[6] We may be reduced to metaphors and models (where theology is concerned), in other words, and our criterion of truth may be largely pragmatic, but that does not mean that there is no truth to be found.

But just how does God interact with human beings and with the world? We saw in chapter one what a sticking point this question is for traditional theism: how can God be said to interact at all with God's cosmos without violating absolutely fundamental scientific principles such as the conservation of energy and the law of entropy? First of all, McFague uses her metaphors and models to evoke a decidedly immanent deity. The world itself, the universe, is the very "body of God." And with this immanentist model as a center of gravity, McFague can go on to use the models of God as "mother," "lover," and "friend." Each of these metaphors/models should be understood not as referring simply to the relationship between God and the self but, rather, as suggesting the relation between God, the universe, and the whole community of living things. McFague's social consciousness means that she will always connect this vision of the divine with a particular concern for ecology—for nature and the physical universe—and for the disadvantaged and oppressed.[7]

Now we have the background for McFague's concrete claims about divine action within the world. God is immanent; the world is God's body. God relates to the universe like a mother, a lover, a friend. What, exactly, are the implications of these models for the notion of divine agency? McFague pictures God not as intervening from without, a hand reaching out of some other dimension of space and time and manipulating our own reality, but as immanent Spirit:

> God is not primarily the orderer and controller of the universe but its source and empowerment, the breath that enlivens and energizes it. . . . [Spirit theology] does not

claim that the divine mind is the cause of what evolutionary theory tells us can have only local causes; rather, it
suggests that we think of these local causes as enlivened
and empowered by the breath of God. . . . The principal
reason, then, for preferring spirit to alternative possibilities is that it underscores the connection between God
and the world as not primarily the Mind that orders, con-
trols, and directs the universe, but as the Breath that is the
source of life and vitality.[8]

When it comes to one particular arena of God's possible agency
vis-a-vis the world, namely biological evolution, McFague fully
acknowledges the tragic waste in the evolutionary story and the
total absence of teleology from the scientific perspective. But she
holds that the arrival of human beings on the scene means that
we can now add purpose to the direction of the cosmos through
our own way of being. And she claims that it is possible to experience divine direction in human life, direction not of a biological
sort, but rather of an existential kind: individual human beings can
experience and have experienced salvific, healing power in their
lives. On this basis, she would like to read teleology back into the
cosmos. Yet she does so in a highly qualified (perhaps "fictional"?)
fashion:

> . . . what does it mean to say that salvation is the *direc-
> tion* of creation and creation is the *place* of salvation? . .
> . It is a statement of faith in the face of massive evidence
> to the contrary, evidence that we have suggested when
> we spoke of the absurdity of such a claim in light of both
> conventional standards and natural selection. Some nat-
> ural theologies, theologies that begin with creation, try
> to make the claim that evolutionary history contains a
> teleological direction, an optimistic arrow, but our claim
> is quite different. It is a retrospective, not a prospective
> claim; it begins with salvation, with experiences of lib-
> eration and healing that one wagers are from God, and
> reads back into creation the hope that the whole creation

is included within the divine liberating, healing powers. It is a statement of faith, not of fact; it takes as its
standpoint a concrete place where salvation has been
experienced—in the case of Christians, the paradigmatic
ministry of Jesus. . . . [9]

McFague's work offers much promise for the harmonizing of theology and science: she suggests a model of God as empowering the
universe from within rather than of God intervening from without.
And the teleology that she finds in creation is one self-consciously
read onto the cosmos on the basis of human experiences of healing
and salvation.

Yet, what McFague provides is what might well be called a
stepping-stone to a genuine melding of theology and science, for
there are still problems with her stance, at least if we take it at face
value. First, her talk of God as empowering Spirit of the universe
remains metaphorical or a model. It may be that our lack of knowledge limits us to metaphor and model, but to engage the scientific worldview seriously, we must be able to explain in more literal
terms at least something of what this claim means (models, at least,
have a conceptual component). In any case, it is a claim that, while
avoiding the old-fashioned interventionist model of God's relationship to the universe, may remind some readers of the decidedly
unscientific notion of vitalism. Science can understand the dyna-
mism of the universe and the wonder of life purely in terms of the
categories supplied by physics, chemistry, and biology; it does not
need the added idea of a vitalistic force. That idea was buried a long
time ago, and it ought not to be disinterred now.

Furthermore, even the kind of existential experience of salvific, healing action that McFague describes in the last quotation
above, a kind of action that she subsequently projects (at least by
way of analogy) upon the larger universe, gets us back to the problem focused upon in chapter one. That is, even if God acts "within"
us, within our thinking and feeling and experiencing and interpreting, there will be required the introduction of energy from outside the closed system of purely physical cause and effect. Recall,
in fact, that our central example in chapter one had to do with

my mood shifting from despair to confidence. Even that kind of mental experience, as "existential" and "immanent" as it is, cannot be understood in terms of divine agency, unless we wish to violate the law of conservation of energy.

But suppose that we now push McFague's claim that theology is mostly fiction (a strategy that may be in some tension with the reassurance issued above that she is, finally, a critical realist—she will come out more as a radical pragmatist where theological assertions are concerned—but a strategy that will not at all suggest that purely *scientific* assertions are mostly fiction). What if we take the most radical possible interpretation of her stance? Most all human beings, at least those who are spiritually attuned to their surroundings and social relationships, experience moments of healing and insight, moments that help them construct a healthy vision about the possible direction of their lives. These are experienced as moments of "grace," in that they are often unexpected and, to some extent, inexplicable gifts. This graciousness is given metaphorical expression by referring the experiences to God's action: talk of God's empowering the experiences is, then, an expression of the *existential quality* of the experiences, not of their *causal origin*. On the basis of such healing experiences, we can and ought to construct narratives of our lives that suggest a telos that puts us in a happy and expansive relationship to our fellow human beings and the larger universe. To the extent that we are, indeed, sensitively attuned to the world of relationships that constitute our very being—human beings are not, in fact, monadic Cartesian subjects but always engaged with their natural and social environments—we can utilize metaphors as lenses that project our personal, constructed telos upon that larger world. After all, as McFague points out, human action within the world does have the power to impart a healing telos to the larger universe: our own individual narratives serve as patterns for our action within the world and thus, in a modest sense at least, take the whole universe of which we are a part up into that telos.

Read in this admittedly radical fashion, McFague's theology suggests that talk of the Spirit of God empowering the universe—talk that is metaphorical in *any* reading—is a symbolic way of describing our possible place within the universe, our ability to participate with the larger universe in a project that strives toward healing and wholeness. This immanent, empowering spirit of God is visible only to the eyes of faith, in the sense that it is actualized only when human beings utilize their own individual experiences of healing as cues to take up a particular stance toward the reality of which they are an inextricable part, that is, only when persons have the sensitivity or "faith" both to see their connection with all that is and their responsibility to engage it in the salvific quest.

But what, exactly, does this most radical reading of McFague's theology accomplish? Is her empowering God now entirely a fiction, and, if so, what is this notion of God good for? Here, in other words, we encounter one of the difficult issues raised in the previous chapter, namely, that it may often appear as if radical theology purchases consistency with science at the cost of totally enervating the concept of God (though we should recall that it is part of the very nature of radical theology to eschew God as a personal being, a self-conscious agent who acts upon God's creation in the way in which human beings can act upon their world).

In truth, this radicalized reading of McFague's account of God's relationship to the world provides a potent and effective symbol. Indeed, it possesses great *pragmatic* truth. First of all, it not only *expresses* how the individual who has experienced personal healing can choose to connect that experience to the whole universe, it also powerfully *reinforces* that notion of connection. That is, the metaphor of the empowering spirit of God bespeaks the quester's sense of being bound to the universe and her fellow creatures. But contemplation of the metaphor also strengthens that sense. Furthermore, it inspires the quester to action: the metaphor impels us to take up our own teleological trajectory and do the hard work of attaching it to the universe. We are empowered to work on behalf of all that is, to work for the kind of salvific trajectory that we have experienced in our individual lives. In this sense, the metaphor or symbol of the empowering spirit of God is, in Clifford Geertz's justly famous terminology, not just a symbol *of* the teleology that we can help impart to the cosmos but also a symbol *for* that all-important task, an energizing template. It might well be argued that this most radical reading of McFague's theology passes her own pragmatic test: it does not simply repeat assertions of the Christian tradition handed down from the past but effectively articulates the truth of Christian faith for the present, scientifically informed cultural situation. It is true to that situation at the same time that, while avoiding ancient formulas, it keeps faith with the salvific spirit of the Christian tradition.

But couldn't one have a sense of connection with others and the cosmos, and even of one's duty to impart a healing telos to all that is, without employing any religious symbols at all? Why not just hold to this vision of the world and our place in it as a function of purely secular values? This question is relevant not simply to our consideration of McFague but to the whole enterprise of radical theology. I suggest that without God-symbolism—or some other decidedly spiritual symbolism—it is difficult to keep concretely before one's mind such an *encompassing* vision and such an *optimistic* goal. What is more, really to embrace the way of being that McFague has in mind surely requires a *disciplined spirituality*. Merely to hold that I am connected to all that exists and that I ought to take up the universe into a salvific telos in my actions is to embrace laudable convictions, but ones that will always threaten to remain but a sentimental patina on my general worldview. Really to do the hard work that McFague has in mind, both the hard work of actually experiencing, twenty-four hours a day, my connectedness with what is and the hard work of living in such a way as to take the world up into a salvific telos, seems to require something more than mere intellectual conviction. It requires that I structure my life day by day in such a fashion that my beliefs and responsibilities are truly internalized and actualized. It is akin to learning one of the martial arts: one must make the moves over and over again until one has become so well trained that the moves become natural and fully integrated into one's very being. It is just this sort of training that religious or spiritual devotion provides, and such religious or spiritual dedication is made possible, is given a vivid and concrete focus, by God-talk. In other words, the traditional notions associated with the word *God* are referenced here, but not in a literal fashion. Instead, they are used as symbols that can provide concrete objects of consciousness standing in for abstract ideas such as taking the world up into one's own experience of a salvific telos.

Mary Daly's Depth of Being

That Mary Daly is a radical theologian is a fact that no one should bother disputing. She is radical both in her feminism—her socio-political stance—and in her vision of the divine. Though the two components of her radicalism cannot be entirely separated, it is the latter that is of primary concern to us here. Yet, the former may initially appear to make a connection with science difficult. Daly explains, for instance, that

> there is a disorder at the core of patriarchal consciousness which is engendered by phallocentric myths, ideologies, and institutions. This disorder implies a state of discon-nection from Biophilic [characterized by love of living things] purposefulness, exemplified in such atrocities as the worldwide rape and massacre of women and of the Third World and the destruction of the planet itself.[10]

To the extent that natural science is connected with the patriarchal Western history that Daly condemns, we may find ourselves back at the notion of science as Baconian torture of nature, a sadistic tool to force nature to give up her secrets.

Things look up, however, when we consider Daly's essentially "pantheistic" vision of the divine.[11] Granted, Daly's description of the feminist religious quest is highly metaphorical, with many of the metaphors being of Daly's own creation. These metaphors are undeniably powerful and moving, but if we were left with only these sometimes extravagant expressions—"Self-centering Spinsters whirl around the axis of our own be-ing, and as we do so, matter/spirit becomes more subtle/supple"—we might be at a conceptual and theoretical loss.[12] But there is enough straightforward descrip-tion in Daly's work to make it clear that she embraces a variation of Paul Tillich's notion of God (or Goddess, as the case may be for feminists) as Being-itself. In this scenario, the divine is not a super-natural being beyond the physical universe, indeed not a being of any kind at all. Tillich goes so far as to say that, strictly speaking, God does not "exist," since existence is a property of beings: God is not a being, one being among others, but the "power" or "ground" or "depth" of being that allows beings to be. In Daly's own words, "Be-ing is the verb that says the dimensions of depth in all verbs, such as intuiting, reasoning, loving, imaging, making, acting, as well as the couraging, hoping, and playing that are always there when one is really living."[13]

By its very nature, this power of being embraces all that is, including every dimension of the physical cosmos of concern to science. The feminist spiritual seeker attuned to this depth of being will find herself engaged in "Dis-covering the lost thread of connectedness within the Cosmos and repairing this thread in the process" (perhaps somewhat akin to the Jewish notion of *tikkun*, the act of helping God to repair God's universe).[14]

There is clearly an opening here for connecting radical spirituality and science. This is especially true in that Daly's use of Tillich's notion of the divine as being-itself can be interpreted (perhaps constructively reinterpreted) not as an absolutely mysterious metaphysical force, nor as anything remotely vitalistic (recall our reservations about McFague's work), but rather as a *relation*. That is, being-itself can be construed as a particular sort of connection *enacted by the spiritually astute quester*, a connection among the quester, other persons and living things, and the larger cosmos.[15] Being-itself, then, is spun out of women's own acts of harmonization: "Breathing in harmony with the Elements, we become Con-creators of the Expanding Presence of Be-ing."[16] While Daly herself may not spell out being-itself as essentially relationship in exactly the fashion I have done here, nor speculate on how this notion of divinity could fruitfully be put in dialogue with natural science, her work is certainly suggestive in this regard. The God or Goddess at least dimly glimpsed here could be enriched by scientific knowledge of the cosmos. It would not violate scientific principles, given that it is a relationship rather than some sort of occult force or entity. Yet, it would not simply be consistent with science; it would be a source of spiritual fulfillment for those who embraced it. Surely, we find another stepping-stone here to the melding of science and radical theology.

Gordon Kaufman's Serendipitous Creativity

The perspective of Harvard theologian Gordon Kaufman fits almost seamlessly into our discussion of radical theology. Kaufman is unapologetically radical in his theological thinking, and he goes so far as to identify "God" with what is essentially the evolutionary dynamic uncovered by contemporary science. Kaufman, like McFague, is basically a pragmatist in his theological method. He explains that he wishes to provide "a wider and deeper (pragmatic) framework" for grasping and dealing with human life, the world and God,[17] deeper and wider, that is, than what is offered by traditional Christian theism.

Traditional theism assumes, of course, that its God-talk refers in a mostly realistic fashion to a supreme being who is really "out there" independent of humanity, a supernatural consciousness who has created the universe and continues to act within it, especially to help his creatures.[18] But Kaufman is radically critical about this tradition's assumptions about the nature of our God-talk. While for the tradition, such God-talk is a mirror-like reflection of what God shows us of himself—even if, as St. Paul would have it, we see "through a glass darkly"—for Kaufman, theology is "imaginative construction through and through."[19] Our constructed God-concept, says Kaufman, "sums up, unifies, and represents . . . what are taken to be the highest and most indispensable human ideals and values."[20] This God-concept should serve both to humanize us, to push us forward in our never-ending quest for a richer humanity, and also to relativize all of our finite endeavors: it stands beyond us as something toward which we strive, but, that we ought never to have the hubris to suppose is totally within our puny reach.

But what, more precisely, is the *content* of this value-laden God-concept? Kaufman decides, in his later work, that our notion of God should lead us "consciously to attend to that which, in the evolutionary and historical processes that provide the context of human existence (as we understand it), gives us our humanity and will draw us on to a more authentic humanness."[21] His

God-concept would have us focus upon "the serendipitous creativity manifest in evolutionary and historical trajectories of various sorts."[22] We are back, in essence, to McFague's common creation story (which Kaufman does, in fact, reference in his work). Kaufman knows, as does McFague, that Darwinian evolution shows no hint of purpose or telos. The human species is only one of millions of results of the multi-faceted evolutionary story, and most species produced by evolution have gone extinct. Yet, also like McFague, Kaufman is still sufficiently formed by the larger Christian tradition that he cannot help but introduce what one might call "wagers" that perhaps the evolutionary process has some larger humanizing dynamic about it after all. We shall, for our purposes, bracket these "small steps of faith" that temper Kaufman's radicalism and compromise his embrace of what contemporary science reveals about the world.[23] Of course, where historical forces are concerned, human beings can indeed make an impact, thereby introducing a teleological element, much as McFague suggests in her discussion of how our actions shape the world.

One potentially puzzling element in Kaufman's theology is his insistence that our God-construction points to, or is somehow itself characterized by, deep mystery. Indeed, Kaufman's most thorough exposition of this theology is titled *In Face of Mystery*. There is nothing particularly mysterious, of course, about the notion of that collection of virtues that most effectively leads to our humanization, nor is there anything ultimately mysterious about the idea of the evolutionary process with which Kaufman wishes to link the humanizing (and relativizing) dynamic. But perhaps there always exists a sense, not of straightforward *cognitive* mystery, but of "existential mystery."[24] That is to say, the whole God-project is about the search for meaning and purpose for both the individual and the whole human community. The mystery is that we can never be sure that what we have chosen as the object of our commitment, our "ultimate concern" as Paul Tillich would put it, actually can provide the requisite sense of meaning and purpose. In this sense the universe itself, including the serendipitous evolutionary process that led to *Homo Sapiens*, is mysterious, for we cannot be certain that it can deliver the existential pay-off that we so badly want. This existential mysteriousness is, for Kaufman, an appropriate characteristic of the search for "God." It is worthwhile to note, too, that it is consistent with the theme of the *risk* of religious commitment emphasized by Soren Kiergekaard and other thinkers in Kaufman's own Protestant tradition.

Kaufman, then, provides us with a theological vision similar to McFague's, though he talks, as even one of his book titles would have it, about constructing the *"concept"* of God, not only about metaphors and models of God.[25] Kaufman, like McFague, concentrates upon the common creation story provided by science, and he focuses on that particular portion of it concerned with the evolutionary movement resulting in human beings. And Kaufman also provides his readers the favor of showing how his theology has implications for two very concrete challenges facing the human race, namely, the prospect of nuclear annihilation and of ecological disaster.[26]

Ursula Goodenough's Divine Mystery

In his influential book of 1917, *Das Heilige*, translated into English as *The Idea of the Holy*, Rudolf Otto describes religious experience as experience of a *mysterium tremendum et fascinans*. The divine is a mystery that is at once attractive and overpowering, indeed overpowering to the extent that it instills a sense of fear in those who are confronted by it. It is a *tremendum* that fills the mind with "blank wonder," producing in us the "creature feeling," the recognition that we are mere, fragile creatures before the mighty, infinite force that has brought us into being.[27] Cell biologist Ursula Goodenough is well acquainted with the *tremendum*, which she associates with a panic-inducing college-aged experience of looking up at the vast, starry heavens.[28] As an adult and a scientist, she has since overcome the sense of terror that the cosmos induced in that experience. But she still finds the world of nature, from the Big Bang to the evolution of life on earth, a source of intense wonder and, sometimes, of mystery (the sort of *"existential* mystery" emphasized by Kaufman, one would think). That radical theologies can point to something that evokes a tremendous sense of wonder, a sense that is well-nigh overpowering, is of the greatest significance. Too often, radical theologies have evinced something so rarified and abstract that, far from evoking a sense of the *tremendum*, they have appealed only to the intellect, and even then only to the intellects of a very few.[29]

In Goodenough's case, the sense of mystery and wonder leads not to the search for some supernatural or transcendent designer, but to the most straightforwardly radical theology of the four considered here, namely, to what she terms "religious naturalism." That is, Goodenough's religious vision is a form of naturalism and thus eschews *any* nonphysical spiritual forces or entities: the philosophy of reality at work here is the matter-energy worldview of natural science. Life itself, which many persons are wont to find the most mysterious of all phenomena studied by science, receives a sober treatment by Goodenough:

> all of us, and scientists are no exception, are vulnerable to the existential shudder that leaves us wishing that the foundations of life were something other than just so much biochemistry and biophysics . . . the workings of life are not mysterious at all. They are obvious, explainable, and thermo-dynamically inevitable. And relentlessly mechanical. And bluntly deterministic. My body is some 10 trillion cells. Period.[30]

But this hardly means that the scientific account of life leaves us with no footholds for spirituality. On the contrary, Goodenough has a great deal to say about our self-transcending interconnection with other living things (and the dynamic of participation and self-transcendence will be crucial in the latter portions of this chapter). It is a connection that Goodenough wishes to celebrate: "Blessed be the tie that binds. It anchors us. We are embedded in the great evolutionary story of planet Earth, the spare, elegant process of mutation and selection and bricolage. And this means that we are anything but alone."[31] Indeed, Goodenough goes so far as to underline the spiritual relevance of this sense of interconnectedness by pointing out that the etymology of the word *religion* takes us back to the Latin *religio*, which means "to bind together."[32]

Goodenough wishes self-consciously to participate in the world of nature revealed by science. The scientific account of nature is relevant to our very identity: "In order to give assent to who we are, we need to understand who we are."[33] And, she says, "I have come to understand that the self, my self, is inherently sacred. By virtue of its own improbability, its own miracle, its own emergence."[34]

But precisely because life and nature are sometimes frighteningly other and without Design, to affirm our place in the larger web of nature is to engage in a potent form of participation and self-transcendence. We learn to affirm that "What Is, Is."[35] This self-transcendence includes the ability to affirm a natural order that dictates that we must die. A single-celled organism can, in theory, go on and on if only it continues to find favorable environmental conditions. But multicellularity brings with it the phenomenon of death. For in multicellular beings, it is the germ cells, the cells responsible for reproduction, that are set up for immortality: they can pass their genetic material to future generations. But the other cells in the organism are specialized and assigned other tasks, and thereby forgo immortality, which means that the organism as a whole must forgo it too. To look foursquare at nature, including at our mortality, and to affirm its sacred character, is to manage a fundamental sort of self-transcendence. Goodenough's religious naturalism is impressive for many reasons, not least because of its bracing realism about nature, its ability to forge a potent spirituality despite taking the infamous dictum of physicist Steven Weinberg—the more we learn about the universe, the more pointless it seems—with utmost seriousness.

Reforming Theism Radically

This survey of four thinkers relevant to our quest for a scientifically-informed radical theology has found theologians whose positions manifest all six of the qualities of radical theology listed in chapter two: they all emphasize an immanent God or Goddess; they draw upon scientific reasoning and knowledge and not simply upon tradition and dogma to form their theologies, as is especially evident in Kaufman's theology based on evolution; they are universalist in their consideration of spiritual resources, as when Daly appropriates the Egyptian goddess Isis; they are committed to the contemporary worldview, as in McFague's focus upon the "common creation story"; and they are humanistic, as evidenced in the pragmatic dynamic in McFague's and Kaufman's works which leads them to suppose that they are in touch with the "true" God when that God provides an impetus toward social justice.

Having briefly surveyed the science-friendly positions of four contemporary radical religious thinkers, we are now in a position to draw upon their insights as we attempt to provide the outlines of a scientifically informed pantheism. This task demands that we start with a brief description of the human subject. Philosophers from Soren Kierkegaard to Martin Heidegger have recognized that the human person is not a fixed entity, but, rather, an activity. More specifically, the self is the activity of synthesis. In Heidegger's epochal *Being and Time*, the self is the act of temporal synthesis, a putting together of the remembered past with the present moment and the projected future. This synthesis is not accidental or haphazard: it is a function of the individual subject's care or *Sorge* for the meaning-world in which she finds herself. This is not "care" in the sense of loving-kindness, but rather the more generalized notion of concern with particular projects that I have in the world. This temporal synthesis powered by care highlights the fact that the human way of being is never the being of an isolated subject, a "monad without windows" in the Leibnitzian phrase, but rather always being-in-the-world. Heidegger's synthesis of past, present, and future, that transcends any single now-point, is designated *finite* transcendence inasmuch as it is tied to the finitude of temporality.

Heidegger's sketch of the human way of being can be expanded, for our purposes, by suggesting that a crucial activity of the human person is *participation and self-transcendence*. John Donne's famous dictum that "no man is an island" is surely on the mark, for we are all characterized by being-in-the-world, that is, meaningful participation in persons, objects, forces, and ideas outside ourselves. This participation brings with it self-transcendence: every new act of participation takes the self at least one step beyond where it previously found itself. Via participation, the self is richer and more experienced. Participation allows for what Nietzsche called "self-overcoming" (even if not in the particular fashion tied to Nietzsche's philosophy of the will to power).

But not all acts of participation and self-transcendence can be accurately designated "finite transcendence." Kierkegaard maintained that the act of synthesis that the self puts together includes not only the poles of actuality and possibility, but also of time and eternity and of finitude and infinitude. Of course, there are theological assumptions built into Kierkegaard's analysis from the start. But even if we do not begin with a decidedly theological agenda, we can acknowledge that there are different forms of self-transcendence effected by our participation in the world. On the one hand, there are the small steps in the process of self-overcoming that are made possible by our daily being-in-the-world. But, on the other hand, there are also acts of participation with their resultant form of self-transcendence that might well become the focus of what Paul Tillich calls "ultimate concern," a notion mentioned in our discussion of Gordon Kaufman. My merely day-to-day concerns, my "care" about my discrete acts in my world, do not rise to the level of ultimacy. Ultimate concern, says Tillich, is concern about that which determines my being and non-being. Tillich has in mind not simply my physical existence or non-existence, but the whole meaning of my being and my ability courageously to maintain it over against all of the threats against it, from death to guilt to the anxiety of emptiness.

Practically speaking, whatever serves as my ultimate concern, that which provides the basis for my courage to be, that which allows me to hold onto a meaningful existence in spite of the threats against it, is God for me. Obviously, some choices, that people actually make when it comes to ultimate concerns—the German hyper-nationalism that was Nazism, for example—are bad choices indeed. But what each of the four representative radical theologians considered here maintain, in one fashion or another, is that there are aspects of the natural world uncovered by contemporary science that can effectively function as my ultimate concern. Granted, *all* human activity and meaning-generation is dependent, in the end, on the principles, particles, fields, and other phenomena uncovered by science. But we are thinking here of the power of *self-conscious reflection upon* what science reveals. Mary Daly is concerned with a "being-itself" that we have read as a relation enacted between human beings and the universe. Sallie McFague clearly draws many of her metaphors and models for the divine from the natural universe, and, in our radical tweaking of her thought, the divine need not be something more that stands behind the cosmos as its supernatural creator. Gordon Kaufman stakes his claim to ultimacy by looking to a particular evolutionary dynamic in the universe. Finally, Ursula Goodenough looks entirely straightforwardly to the natural cosmos as the source of ultimate inspiration.

From the perspective of a radical theology, there is no objective calculus for determining just which ultimate concern, if, indeed, there be just one, is the correct one. But Daly—or at least our version of her thought—McFague, Kaufman, and Goodenough all wager that the universe revealed to us by modern science is a fully legitimate candidate for our ultimate source of orientation in life. Surely, there are good reasons for this wager. The natural cosmos is, after all, the source of everything that is, including our own existence. It confronts us with overpowering grandeur and alluring intellectual riddles. Given the problems plaguing traditional theism laid out in chapter one, a theology focused upon science and the cosmos seems all the more reasonable and attractive.

A Cosmocentric Turn

To acknowledge that the natural cosmos can bear the weight of ultimate concern is to endorse something that can accurately be regarded as a form of pantheism or panentheism. Recall that the former equates God directly with the whole of reality, with the universe, while the latter thinks of the universe as part of God's being, which also transcends the universe. In what follows, I shall lean more toward pantheism, while some of the radical theologians we have considered above, such as McFague and Kaufman, might be more comfortable with panentheism. More exactly, I will argue that the natural cosmos in the particular garb that it wears when viewed from the perspective of contemporary science deserves the pragmatic appellation "God." Even the most rudimentary sort of analysis, one focused upon the Big Bang, bolsters this contention.

The latest data from investigations of the cosmic background radiation, a telltale signature left behind by the Big Bang, suggests that our universe came to birth approximately 13.7 billion years ago. Hence, we are already confronted by an overpowering vastness, a *tremendum*, in this case a vastness of time, which is augmented by the universe's present spatial vastness. Furthermore, although this event has no mark of having been designed or having issued from purposeful action—perhaps design is actually ruled out here *a priori*, since the Big Bang is bound to the principle of quantum indeterminacy—it is nonetheless of immediate spiritual import for human beings, for it is one of our most basic intellectual predilections to ask from whence we came. Even on the level of my individual biography, if I was adopted as a child, for instance, I will wonder who my birth parents were and what they were like, for the issue of origin, whether purposeful or not, is inextricably linked to identity. I am who I am, in large part, as a function of where I am "located" in the larger scheme of things. And to understand that *everything* began 13.7 billion years ago in the Big Bang is to catch a glimpse of that all-important larger scheme of things.

How, then, does this scientific insight into our origin provide an opportunity for participation and self-transcendence?[36] Most obviously, it does so by dramatically demonstrating that we are radically dependent on something far different from ourselves and our own human powers. We, and everything else that exists, depend, ultimately, on that singular explosion of space-time out of the vacuum. And such dependence is, after all, a dramatic instance of participation. If the great nineteenth-century Reformed theologian Friedrich Schleiermacher, the "father of modern Protestant theology," was on the right track in defining religion as the self-consciousness of absolute dependence, then we may well take up a religious attitude toward the universe's originary event.[37] Of course, if we are honest with ourselves, we must acknowledge that this event on which all beings are dependent did not bring us into existence out of any conscious desire to do so. The Big Bang is not an expression of beneficence. As a result, one may question why I would want to cultivate a sense of participation in the forces or force that precipitated the Big Bang and why I would wish to hone my sense of dependence upon it. What spiritual benefit can I possibly derive from developing a sense of participation and dependence on something that is, in fact, simply unaware of me and of the rest of humanity?

There are at least two pertinent responses to this question. First, it will be recalled that we seek participation—even, or perhaps especially, in the form of the sense of dependence—in order to achieve self-transcendence. We step outside ourselves, beyond the ordinary confines of our ego, in order to achieve an expansive selfhood, or (as in some of the Asian traditions) something beyond ego and selfhood altogether. The recognition of our radical dependence, via the dependence of literally everything that is, on the Big Bang can certainly effect a powerful experience of self-transcendence, of stepping outside the confines of one's present ego.

Second, just as we must be careful not to anthropomorphize the origin of the universe by projecting onto it something such as intention or beneficence, so too we must avoid the frequent mistake of writing off the religious significance of events such as the Big Bang because they are "indifferent" to the human project. The use of the notion of indifference in this context turns out to be another instance of projection. How is the word *indifferent* or *indifference* used in ordinary parlance, that is, in the contexts that manifest the basic meaning of the word? It is, of course, a human being that is indifferent: "I mentioned going to the movies, but Sal was indifferent to the idea." *Indifference*, in other words, suggests that a person does not care for or about something. Thus, the word can take on a negative moral tone if it is applied in the context of reacting to the needs of other persons: "Jack was indifferent to Frank's pleas for help, though Jack had always professed to be Frank's friend."

Herein lies the danger, then: to say that the universe is indifferent to the human project may be intended merely to suggest that the universe has no consciousness at all about humanity, but the deeper resonance of that assertion is usually that the universe is a cold, dark place that has chosen to turn its back on us. But, of course, this is just as inaccurate as any claim that the universe is kindly disposed to us. The Big Bang and the universe are neither gracious to us nor indifferent to us. But they are, in any case, that upon which we are thoroughly dependent for both our origin and our continued existence. As such, contemplation of them can launch the ego on a trajectory that takes it far beyond its ordinary state of self-absorption.

Pantheism and Theism

Let us think in a bit more detail about how this might work by contrasting it with the traditional theistic approach. In the latter perspective, God as a personal Supreme Being is the object of my ultimate concern. Note how this addresses my desire for participation and self-transcendence. God has created the world with a particular purpose in mind, a purpose for humanity in particular. I participate in this divine plan through faith, which provides me with a potent sense of meaning and purposefulness in life. It is a meaning that already exists in the mind of God; I need only discover it, not create it. What is more, God has created me precisely so that this meaning, and nothing else, will fulfill my being.

When we turn to a pantheism focused upon nature as described by science, we are, of course, not dealing with a supreme mind. There can be no prearranged meaning, since meaning is always a function of consciousness. What happens, then, is that I decide that the universe taken as a whole can *become* a potent source of meaning, one worthy of being called religious, if I decide to approach it in a particular way. I seek participation and self-transcendence; hence, I choose to understand myself, to narrate the story of my life, in terms of my place within the cosmos. I am tied to that larger cosmos, after all, by the host of laws and constants that hold it together. And to understand myself as a cosmic being is to experience a particularly powerful form of self-transcendence. Now I am who I am as one located within the larger milieu of all that is, where that milieu is not a chaos, but an intelligible whole.

But how, exactly, should a scientifically articulated pantheism be embraced? What would it mean, in practical terms, to make the universe so conceived one's ultimate concern? The first thing to be noted is that my sense of participating in the cosmos that originated nearly 14 billion years ago in the Big Bang is not unmediated. In my most emotionally charged experiences of participation in the cosmos, it might *seem* to me that the relation being actualized is between the natural universe and myself alone. But, in fact, that sense of being a monadic individual facing the cosmos is an illusion, for everything that I know about the cosmos is dependent upon the other human beings with whom I interact throughout my life. It is the thoroughly communal project of scientific investigation, after all, with its emphasis on replication of experiment by different individuals, that has provided the specific lens through which my scientifically articulated pantheism views the universe. And, even more fundamentally perhaps, my ability to enjoy the contemplation of the universe presupposes that my basic needs—my health and safety, for example—have all been seen to. That presupposes my place within a society.

Thus, it is that the project of pantheistic participation is built upon a more immediate kind of participation and self-transcendence, namely, the one that takes place in my relationships with my fellows. There is something pragmatically helpful about this. While I may believe that my awed response to the cosmos calls forth a genuine self-transcendence on my part, how can I be sure that it is not really a mood of self-aggrandizement that results instead? "Look at me: I'm one with the universe!" But my concrete dealings with other human beings provide a check, a test of whether I do live a genuinely self-transcending, self-overcoming existence. He who claims to love God but hates his brother or sister is self-deceived and a liar. So St. John tells us (I John 2: 9-11), and it is still well to heed his warning. Any pantheism worth its salt, then, must be seen as part of the more basic web of self-transcendence created via my social interaction.

It is at this point that we can appropriate some of the insights of Mary Daly, Sallie McFague, Gordon Kaufman, and Ursula Goodenough in order to round out our pantheism. Let us begin with what McFague can offer us. There are two emphases in her theology that are particularly pertinent. First, McFague, it will be recalled, underlines the absolute necessity of metaphors and models in theology. All of our statements about and conceptions of the divine are provisional at best, and all must have the essential character of metaphor: they all combine a small measure of "is" with a large component of "is not." Symbols surely have a place in our scientifically informed pantheism. Actual piety toward the universe requires a concrete object of consciousness, and that points us to symbolism. One of the functions of the American flag is to allow me to think the notion of the American people and nation, a reality that has far too many components for me to grasp directly and literally. Perhaps, then, I can unify the literally innumerable aspects of the universe under the symbol "God." That is, I can use the anthropomorphic notion of deity found in the Jewish and Christian traditions, not as a concept that points literally to an existing supernatural being, but as a symbol that, like the flag, serves as a concrete focus for consciousness that can stand in for everything encompassed by the cosmos. It is essential to note that a major component of the symbolism at issue here is the act of valuation. Theoretically, we could use the symbol of God for purely cognitive purposes, namely, to provide a value-neutral, albeit concrete, content of consciousness to stand in for the constituents of the universe. But it makes much more sense to press the symbol of God into service when we are looking for a way to concretely symbolize the universe in its special role as the object of our ultimate concern, our most cherished values, akin to how the flag concretizes the American nation, *as an object of patriotic devotion*, for consciousness. The great American pragmatist philosopher John Dewey suggested something parallel to our proposal. The notion of God, said Dewey, could be used to stand in for the unity of our ideal ends along with the conditions in nature and society that make the realization of those ideals possible.[38]

Here lies the way to a genuine pan*theism*, even if the theism part of the equation is symbolic. However, not only are there important differences between Dewey's focus on a mono-thematically ethical conception of "God" and our own more multiform use of God-symbolism, but there is also an important difference between Dewey's time and ours. Dewey stood upon a shore that overlooked the "high tide of American liberalism."[39] Our own time is very different. The term *liberalism* here does not mean political liberalism in the sense that, in the United States, the Democratic party tends to be more "liberal" than the Republican. Rather, the term suggests an optimism about human capabilities for moral and intellectual growth through education and scientific investigation that seems naive to many twenty-first-century persons. But if the social milieu into which ideas and convictions are introduced is all-important in determining their power, there is something about our own day and age particularly relevant to the reception of a scientifically informed pantheism. As never before, the general public has a visceral sense of the overpowering grandeur of the cosmos, of its character as *temendum*. Thanks to outer space probes, and most especially the Hubble Space Telescope, we are treated to endless images of fiery nebulae and distant galaxies. They stare out at us from books, magazines, television, and the internet. Far from appealing only to the intellect, then, the natural cosmos today has a hold upon the larger manifold of human capacities and excites a genuine sense of wonder. Hence, despite the tide of liberalism having ebbed since Dewey's time, the particular form of God-symbolism that we are proposing fits nearly seamlessly with the contemporary perception of the material universe.

A second theme that we ought not overlook in McFague is her emphasis on the role of our images of deity in promoting social and ecological justice. Surely, we do participate in something beyond ourselves and attain to at least a cognitive self-transcendence when we understand ourselves as part of the whole history of the cosmos. But, as we noted above in our discussion of the mediated character of the sense of participation in the universe, there is a stronger form of self-transcendence that religions have usually demanded, namely, an ethical self-transcendence in which we give up not only our insular *notion* of self, but actually make concrete sacrifices that translate into action on behalf of others. "Faith without works," the New Testament book of James reminds us, "is dead" (James 2:17). Whether our notions of the divine promote and empower social and ecological justice is, then, a pragmatic test of the potency of the self-transcendence that our God-talk affords. Thus, a scientifically articulated pantheism that stresses our participation in all that exists and a resultant self-transcendence should issue in concrete acts on behalf of the earth and our fellow human beings.

Gordon Kaufman's theology reinforces this perspective. He too is concerned with theology's role in informing a sense of ecological justice. What is more, Kaufman is particularly concerned to call our attention to the religious implications of the evolutionary dynamic that resulted in our own species. While a strict scientific reading of evolution eschews any teleological component, something that Kaufman is tempted to import into his theology, Kaufman surely provides food for thought in his treatment of how, once we human beings have arrived on the evolutionary scene, our evolutionary heritage can be taken up into our projects, thus self-consciously *re-placing* our evolution into a teleological context.

Ursula Goodenough's reflections offer us a great deal of help in continuing to build up our scientifically articulated pantheism. This is true for both content and method. Where content is concerned, Goodenough's treatment of biology, in particular, provides material that can surely enhance the sense of participation and self-transcendence that powers our pantheism. Methodologically speaking, her careful exploration of our very human response to the cosmos, from a sense of the *tremendum* to the practice of Buddhist mindfulness, provides instruction that we can profitably follow in fine-tuning our pantheism. We shall, indeed, attempt to follow Goodenough's instruction in greater detail in chapter five below.

In Mary Daly's case, what is particularly important is her approach to the ontology of the divine. More accurately, what matters most here is our constructive interpretation of that approach. We suggested that Daly's Being is not some independent power that existed before human beings came upon the scene.

Rather, Being—or the divine—is a *relation* that can exist between the self and the universe, a relation that we can *freely choose to enact.* Similarly, our reading of the universe in terms of pantheism is meant to point not to an eternal and immutable deity empowering the cosmos, but, instead, to a relation that can be enacted if and when the individual chooses to attune herself to the world of nature in a particular fashion.

CHAPTER FOUR

A Universe of Things: The Parts and the Whole

We have laid the foundations of a scientifically informed pantheism, one shaped by readings of the work of Sallie McFague, Gordon Kaufman, Mary Daly, and Ursula Goodenough. In some ways, we have pushed the insights of these theologians further than they themselves have done. The resultant pantheism involves participation and self-transcendence focused upon the world described by science. That world is a "universe." We must now think in more detail about what that implies. In what senses, specifically, does the world hang together as a "universe," a unified reality? Our investigation in this chapter will begin with a consideration of the *formal unity* of the cosmos, which can be subdivided into a *cognitive* component—the cognitive dimension has to do with how we grasp things through reason—and a *phenomenological* component—the phenomenological dimension has to do with how things appear to our consciousness—and the *material unity of the cosmos*, which subdivides into *ontological*—the ontological dimension has to do with the actual being of the thing we know—along with *cognitive* and *enacted* components.

The Unity of the Universe

There is, first of all, a *formal* unity to reality, one that does not involve reference to any of the specific parts that make it up. In the *cognitive* sphere we encounter the idea or concept of the universe as the set of all the things that exist. The universe, in other words, is what is, without specifying any of the particular things that exist.

Phenomenologically, and equally formally, the universe is *the* objective correlate of our consciousness, that which is intended by our consciousness. More exactly, it is the whole of what can be intended. Intended reality is unified, is one, just insofar as consciousness is one.

But the universe is not simply a formal whole, but also a *material* whole. It is so, first of all, in that everything that we know of in the physical universe that we inhabit is held together by a single interlocking set of constants and laws. Because the universe is characterized in and of itself by these constants and laws, the unity at issue here is *ontological*.

However, insofar as science allows us to understand the relevant constants and laws and how they hold physical reality together, we also have the opportunity *cognitively* to grasp the universe's material unity.

Enacted Unity

There is a third way in which material unity can be conferred upon the reality in which we find ourselves. This is a matter of *enacted unity*, something we have touched upon several times in our treatment of Mary Daly. Let us investigate this particularly significant form of unity in greater detail, by reference to the Anthropic and the Poetic Cosmological Principles.

The Anthropic Cosmological Principle serves as our point of departure.[1] The word *anthropic* comes from the Greek word for "man," the same root from which we get the term *anthropology*. The Anthropic Principle, then, focuses on the manner in which the universe seems fine-tuned for human life. Without a bevy of surprisingly exact constants on the atomic and subatomic levels, matter could not form at all, and life would thus be impossible. On the macroscopic scale, it is intriguing to note that the earth is in just the right place vis-à-vis the sun to support life, that the moon stabilizes the earth so that its climate has remained constant enough for life to evolve, and that Jupiter appears to sweep away large space rocks that would otherwise have a significant chance of slamming into the earth and halting any development of life.[2] It may even turn out that the much-discussed "dark energy" that some scientists now suppose accounts for the universe's accelerated expansion had to have just the value it does in order for galaxies, stars, and planets—obvious prerequisites for life as we know it—to come into existence.[3]

What should we make of considerations of this sort? The "weak" version of the Anthropic Cosmological Principle answers with the distressingly obvious contention that we would not be here to do science if the universe were not hospitable to human life. The "strong" version of the Anthropic Principle, by contrast, suggests that there are too many fortuitous circumstances simply to dismiss the matter as coincidence. Perhaps we should consider divine design. A more scientifically acceptable choice, according to some cosmologists, is to defuse the apparent unlikelihood of our being here by embracing the notion of multiple universes, or the "multiverse." If our own universe is only one of innumerable universes, each with its own characteristics, then there is nothing so unlikely after all about our world being characterized by a complex web of conditions hospitable to life. If the odds of our particular universe are one in a billion, and there are ten billion universes, then there need be no surprise that we are here.

Of course, we are interested in a more decidedly spiritual principle. Whatever its potential weaknesses, there is one component of the Anthropic Principle—indeed, it is the Principle's defining core—that provides us with a clue as to how we might fill out our pantheism: the Anthropic Cosmological Principle asks us to view the universe from the vantage point of human life. A spirituality and a theology linked to the natural universe must surely do the same, given that spirituality and theology are all about how human beings find fulfillment in life. Hence, let us propose to explore what we shall call the Poetic Cosmological Principle. The English words *poetry* and *poetic* are derived from the Greek word *poiein*, which means "to create" or "to make." We shall encounter an anthropic component, then, not as something uncovered in the structure of the universe just in and of itself, but as something we ourselves bring to the equation. Human beings who, on their spiritual quest, embrace a scientifically informed pantheism engage in a particular sort of creating or making: they create a new form of unity in the cosmos.

To the extent that we are going to *create* unity in the universe in this instance, we obviously do not begin with the universe as an already unified whole. Rather, we seek participation in one or more constituents of the cosmos. Let us suppose that I am meditating upon the beauty of the trees outside my window. The trees upon which I am focusing are instances of nature, that is, of the larger natural world, and by thinking about those trees in relation to the quest for participation and self-transcendence, I unify the trees—and, by extension, the universe of which they are a part and that they represent—around that existential quest. It is akin to the situation artfully described—not insignificantly, in *poetry*—by Wallace Stevens:

> I placed a jar in Tennessee,
> And round it was, upon a hill.
> It made the slovenly wilderness
> Surround that hill.
>
> The wilderness rose up to it,
> And sprawled around, no longer wild.[4]

The jar exerts no gravitational force on the wilderness round about it. Rather, the phenomenon Stevens describes is a perspectival one. Similarly, pantheistic piety is hardly an attempt to manhandle the universe. It is, after all, an act of self-transcendence. The unity effected by pantheism as understood here is, like the unity effected by the jar, a perspectival one. The human quest for meaning provides a unifying vantage point on the cosmos. That this is a unity the cosmos would not possess without the pantheist's quest—just as the Tennessee wilderness would not possess the same unity without the jar placed atop the hill—indicates that the pantheistic quester actually accomplishes something for the universe in her participation and self-transcendence. As it turns out, this is of great importance, for it suggests that pantheistic piety is not simply a matter of one's thinking or attitude, but that it involves a particular kind of doing, of action.

There is a venerable tradition within Western thought according to which, when we contemplate the natural world, we raise what is devoid of awareness to consciousness; nature becomes conscious of itself via our thinking about nature. We can find examples of this sentiment from Augustine to Aquinas. It reaches its philosophical conclusion in the absolute idealism of G. W. F. Hegel. But what we have in mind here is not limited to mere *cognition* of nature and the universe (nor does it carry metaphysical implications in the way that Hegel's philosophy does). It involves cognition along with aesthetic contemplation, longing for self-transcendence, ethical aspiration, and the other components that make up the fullness of human existentiality.

The pantheistic quester can justifiably suppose, then, that her participation in the cosmos is an active, creative undertaking, an exercise in a spiritual poeticizing, in the etymological sense of that term. The Poetic Cosmological Principle bears a resemblance to our radical reading of Sallie McFague's and Gordon Kaufman's on the evolutionary dynamic in the universe. That reading blocked any teleological dimension in the universe except what is imparted by human consciousness.[5] But that consciousness does provide something akin to teleology, and it is a teleology that embraces the entire cosmos. There should be no negative implications attached to calling this a "projected" teleology. The pantheistic quester imparts a teleological dynamic to the universe, but the projection in question is not a Feuerbachian or Freudian one. For those two masters of suspicion—the phrase is Paul Ricouer's (applied to Marx and Freud)—projection is a function of false consciousness and, thus, has destructive results, such as the alienation of the human being from itself. The theistic projection they have in mind deserves Richard Dawkins's appellation "delusion."[6] But, of course, the sort of projection involved in setting the jar of the spiritual quest in the midst of the physical universe is a fully conscious, free, and creative undertaking. In this regard, it is, indeed, akin to the act undertaken by the narrator of Stevens' poem.

How the Poetic Cosmological Principle functions can be further illuminated by seeing it as akin to the role of art in philosopher Hans-Georg Gadamer's monumental *Truth and Method*. We often suppose, as did Immanuel Kant, that, while the natural sciences provide us with *knowledge* of the world, art provides us only with *subjective satisfaction*. Suppose that I am a botanist (even more specifically, for those who demand precision, a dendrologist): I investigate a copse of trees by bringing my scientific acumen to bear upon what I see. Perhaps I will note the soil conditions, the light and shade, and the way in which the trees interact with the underbrush, among other things. Few would deny that my investigation will produce knowledge about the trees in question.

Now imagine that I am a gifted painter. I survey the copse of trees every time that I pass it on my daily hikes through the woods. One day, perhaps with easel in front of the trees, or perhaps in my studio, I paint the trees. If we suppose that the painting is a powerful work of art, what do we imagine that it accomplishes? Surely, it will communicate something of the beauty of the trees, and perhaps even some dimension of my more specific emotional reactions to them. But what about *knowledge*? Isn't that left to the botanist? Not at all, says Gadamer. The work of art is the "raising up of . . . reality into its truth."[7] One way to interpret Gadamer's admittedly cryptic saying here is to suggest that the painting takes what is, in and of itself, an inchoate collection of objects and pulls them together into a patterned whole. That whole provides a meaning-context, what we might actually call a "world," in which the trees can be placed. As part of a world, we can grasp the meaning—or at least some of the meanings—of the trees. That is, my painting has unified the trees, and unified them with my larger meaning-world, so that the painting communicates what the trees mean and thus provides knowledge.[8]

Viewing a work of art, then, might in certain circumstances illustrate the Poetic Cosmological Principle. If the work raises up a portion of reality, the subject matter of the painting, into its truth for me as viewer by unifying it with the larger meaning-universe in which I seek to participate, if, that is, it provides a perspectival unity for the universe that is based upon my ultimate existential concerns, then it helps me to enact a spiritually efficacious harmony among the constituent elements of the universe.[9]

God and the Quest

It was suggested in chapter three that it would prove edifying to symbolize the unity of the universe with the notion of God. That is, in a fashion similar to what John Dewey envisioned, one could take the idea of the Supreme Being and interpret it, not as pointing to an actually existing entity, but as a symbol of the unification of the innumerable existents making up the cosmos. We cannot in any way take into consciousness all those existents. Hence, we can use the symbol of God to stand in for all of them in their unity, much as the American flag stands for 350 million Americans, with the all-important additional consideration that "God" here stands for the unity of the cosmos just insofar as it becomes the object of our ultimate concern. We are now in a position to augment this perspective: the universe becomes the focus of our ultimate concern when we ourselves provide an element of its unity by "poetically" pulling its constituent elements together around our quest for participation and self-transcendence.

A pantheistic spirituality conceived in the foregoing personal fashion—the *individual quester* actually helps to put the unity in the universe as object of ultimate concern—raises an important question: Is there any way in which the "God" of our scientifically informed pantheism can be a *personal* God? The answer is clearly negative if we mean by a personal God an actually existing personal consciousness. We have seen that God is a symbolic construct. And even those who wish to embrace that symbolic construct may feel that part of what is attractive about a scientifically savvy pantheism, especially considering the quest for self-transcendence, is its impersonality. Perhaps I seek to get "lost" in the vastness of what is.

On the other hand, there will always be those spiritual seek-ers who, in the desire to engage their deepest emotional capacities, will want to feel something like love for the object of their ultimate concern. It is difficult, however, to genuinely love, in the fullest sense of the term, an abstraction. While it is always possible to include personal symbolism in one's symbolic God-construct, the knowledge that it is a construct may make a truly loving, personal relationship with it difficult, if not psychologically suspect. This is where the great personal manifestations of the ultimate come into play. What of Jesus, the Buddha, and Krishna? Might it not be possible to fold them into a pantheistic piety, even if there must be an element of symbolic construction here too? No doubt, different questers could come up with a plethora of different ways to carry out such an appropriation. However, I shall propose just one here. It is a way that follows straightforwardly from the nature of the pantheistic piety sketched thus far.

Jesus, the Buddha, and Krishna (to take but one of the many Indian deities) have traditionally been conceived as personal mani-festations of the ultimate, what the Hindus call avatars. In its most conservative form, of course, Buddhism sees the Buddha as only a human teacher. But the doctrine of the Buddhakaya, developed in the Mahayana school of Buddhism, allows the Buddha to join Jesus and Krishna here. It is simple enough for us to say, consistent with what has been worked out above, that Jesus, for example, is a personal manifestation of the pantheistic ultimate. Notice that this is significantly different from saying that Jesus is merely the per-fect exemplar of how we ourselves ought to engage in the process of self-conscious participation in the universe with its attendant self-transcendence. Rather, there is something special about Jesus: Jesus as the Christ incarnates the ultimate itself. There is a ready resource for effecting the approach I have in mind here, at least as old as nineteenth-century Romanticism, in the notion of the human person as a microcosm of the universe, where the universe is the macrocosm. And considered scientifically, one can indeed say that the human person, the most complex entity that we have yet encountered in the universe, literally "embodies" the universe. As with every other entity, the human person exists thanks to the forces and constants that make the universe what it is (at least our corner of the universe, or our universe within the multiverse). To echo the traditional Christian claim that Jesus is God, in the particular context of the pantheism set forth here, is to see in Jesus a uniquely powerful microcosmic manifestation of the universe.[10]

One need not neglect the actual teachings of figures such as Jesus and the Buddha in this approach. Those teachings are, it must be admitted, derived from the vantage point of the seeker approaching the ultimate; here, in other words, Jesus and the Buddha do seem to be simply exemplars, however exceptional, of the spiritual quest upon which any one of us might find herself. The point, however, is that, as incarnations of the ultimate itself, they are much more than that. Let us say that their role as exemplary questers is located within the larger whole of their role as incarnations. In any case, they surely provide a *personal face* for the ultimate. They allow us to grasp the ultimate via the analogy of human personhood and to recognize that ultimate as the source of personhood, as of all else that exists. Hence, just as the Hindu tradition acknowledges the need for a personal face for the inherently trans-personal infinite—the infinite that is "Brahman without qualities"—by providing the yogic path known as *bhakti* yoga, so here figures such as the Buddha and the Christ provide a personal portal to the universe taken as object of spiritual concern. Hence, that immensity that is the universe, our topic at the outset of this chapter, turns out to be available in a personal form that can be engaged with our emotions.

CHAPTER FIVE

Contemplating Your TOE: What Science Offers Radical Spirituality

By looking in the previous chapters at the spiritual dynamic of participation and self-transcendence, we have attained an idea of how radical theology, and the radical spirituality that it serves, can find crucial resources in the scientific worldview. We can participate in the universe(s) revealed by science and, through that sense of participation, attain to a spiritually desirable sort of self-transcendence, one based upon a particular brand of pantheism. Our task in the present chapter, then, is to look in greater and more concrete detail at this process through which science contributes to the spiritual and theological quest. There will be four major sections to our inquiry. First, we shall consider the role of science in providing us with an accurate picture of the universe for our spiritual journey. Second, we shall look at exactly how one can self-consciously participate in particular aspects of the cosmos opened up by contemporary science. Third, the role of TOEs, or "theories of everything," will be examined. Finally, we shall bring the Buddhist notion of mindfulness to bear.

Science and the Religious Quest

In the previous chapters we tacitly embraced an essentially realist attitude to what science shows us about the universe. The scientific perspective is not a mere useful fiction, adopted simply because it happens to serve our "will to power," as Nietzsche would have it. Science is not a parochial invention of a powerful subset of first-world, Western cultures; it provides a perspective that, while, of course, not entirely value-free or simply unaffected by historical and cultural context, has been almost immediately accepted cross-culturally. In short, in a very important sense, science shows us what really is the case about the universe, and it continually makes real progress in adding to the storehouse of genuine human knowledge.

The ability to begin the theological and spiritual quest with this empirically sound, demonstrably accurate account of nature is of inestimable value. Too often in the history of humanity's many religious traditions, theology or its equivalent begins from what can now only be regarded as thoroughly outmoded myths, poetic flights of fancy, or even struggles to maintain social power. Hence, to take each of these three in turn, most traditional religious cosmogonies, stories about the origins of the world, are clearly useless when it comes to understanding the literal details of the origin of the world.[1] It is important to recall, of course, that scholars of religion use the term *myth* in a technical sense, meaning not simply a tall-tale but, rather, a symbolic narrative. The symbolic dimensions of the ancient cosmogonies, which are concerned with what our moral and spiritual place in the universe is, may still be powerful and important.[2] But religious studies scholars know too that the cosmogonies often had, at least for some of their users, in addition to the aforementioned symbolic dimensions, a more straightforward etiological function: they were taken to explain in quite literal terms how things came about. But the spiritual quest and our sense of our place in the larger whole of things can only be skewed by beginning with such misinformed notions of how the world works. Our universe emerged not from a blood-thirsty sea battle between primordial beings, as depicted in the famous Babylonian creation epic, the *Enuma Elish*, but in the Big Bang.

Much of what passes for ancient stories about our place in the cosmos are actually artistic, poetic productions. This is certainly true, for instance, of Homer's accounts of the gods and goddesses. These stories can definitely be appreciated precisely as works of art, but, once again, they provide a faulty initial trajectory for the spiritual quest if they are taken literally to describe the nature of the universe in which we find ourselves.

Finally, even the perennial quest for social power can skew the venerable accounts of the universe found among the world religions. In the nineteenth century, Karl Marx gave unforgettable expression to this fact with his dictum that religion is the "opiate of the people," a drug that pacifies the less fortunate so that they do not rebel against the unjust social order in which they find themselves. A concrete instance, only one among many, is to be found in the traditional notion of the universe in Indian religion. At the beginning of time, according to India's Vedic literature, the gods sacrificed a primordial man. The various parts of that man became the foundations for the layers of the notorious caste system, a strict class system into which one is born and within which one is not allowed to move during this lifetime. The message: the caste system is not a human creation that can be changed but, rather, is built into the very fabric of creation. A religious perspective here serves to prop up what is, from the viewpoint of everyone from the Buddha to Mahatma Gandhi, an unjust social system.

By contrast, natural science, while it may not appear to have any direct implications for spirituality just in and of itself, does us the priceless service of providing an accurate initial orientation for the religious quest. We learn from science how the universe actually began; we learn how we as human beings originated; and we come to understand our relationship to everything else that exists. It is from this vantage point that a quest for meaning, purpose, and moral authenticity can be launched with the best prospects for success. It should be well noted, for instance, that adopting the scientific worldview as the starting point for the spiritual quest simply dissolves hitherto wrenching issues such as the problem of theodicy.

Science and Participation in the Universe

The second major area of study for us in this chapter is the fashion in which science allows for participation in individual facets of the cosmos, as well as the cosmos as a whole. One way in which participation might concretely fit here is illuminated by the perspective of Zen Buddhism. There is a familiar Zen saying that goes this way: "Before I studied Zen, a mountain was a mountain. When I began studying Zen, a mountain was no longer a mountain. When I understood Zen, a mountain was a mountain." That is, before I studied Zen, I took the classification of "mountain" for granted and simply pigeon-holed mountains in the conceptual space our culture usually makes for them. But when I started exploring Zen, that common and unexamined notion of a mountain was problematized, for Zen questions some of our fundamental presuppositions about the world and our tendencies to categorize it in ways that will serve our egotistical purposes. But once I could truly embrace the Zen perspective, I gave up the mental and cultural grids that I formerly laid over mountains; I was now able to see the mountain on its own, just as it is in itself. I saw the mountain in its "simple suchness," that is, just as it is apart from egotistical overlays.

Natural science can perform a parallel service. I begin by inattentively seeing a mountain as just a mountain, as simply what it is in our common cultural understanding. But science complicates things significantly. It forces me to step back and no longer take mountains for granted. Science reveals a dynamic earth with tremendous forces at work, an earth with tectonic plates that shake and move and collide, plates that can push up whole mountain ranges. Having imbibed the insights of geological science, I am enabled to see mountains in a wholly new way, one that is ripe for a sense of participation in the overwhelmingly powerful forces that have formed the surface of the earth.

The three Zen stages are all present here, but let us re-label them for the sake of clarity and coherence with the religious dynamic of participation and self-transcendence. Before I am acquainted with geology, I approach mountains in the spirit of *inattentive use*. I "use" them in the sense that they simply fulfill a particular role within the larger mental grid that I have inherited. In the second stage, when scientific understanding is brought to bear, we initially experience the moment of *"productive distanciation."*[3] That is, geology acquaints me with the highly complex processes that are involved in the formation of a mountain, thereby waking me up, as it were, and distancing me from the spirit of inattentive use. But once I have really imbibed some of the insights of science about mountains, once I have internalized them, then I can see the mountain as what it really is on its own. And this means that, in addition, the mountain becomes a possible object of participation and self-transcendence for me: I have moved to an attitude of *participatory understanding*. It is no longer an object inattentively under my control, but rather something genuinely "other," and that is a prerequisite for the phenomenon of self-transcendence.

The mountain as given to me by science can serve as an object of participation and self-transcendence not just by itself, but also in another way. The mountain can easily stand in for nature as a whole; it is a symbol of the entire cosmos. Thus, through my participation in the mountain, I can understand myself as participating in the universe. The mountain appears throughout humankind's religions as a pointer to the divine, as something with the size, immovability, and proximity to the heavens which have a natural affinity with the notion of the transcendent or the divine. It is no accident that Moses met God and received God's teaching, the Torah, on a mountain, Mount Sinai.

What about specific examples of how science allows us to participate in the cosmos, even to the point of making a scientifically informed pantheism plausible? In chapter three, we considered the spiritual import of contemplating one's origin, along with the origin of everything else that is, in the Big Bang. But other examples can easily be adduced. Consider my relation to the most fundamental building blocks of reality. It used to be supposed that atoms constituted the indivisible units out of which physical reality is made. But then subatomic particles were discovered. We all learned in grade school that, with the exception of hydrogen, atomic nuclei are made out of protons and neutrons. But it turns out that not even protons and neutrons are the end of the road: both are made up of quarks, which are held together by force-carrying particles called, appropriately enough, gluons. Now the majority of quarks in the universe were created a micro-second after the Big Bang. Thus, there are nuclei in the atoms of your body that are made up of quarks nearly as old as the universe itself! This is, potentially, an incredibly powerful avenue to one's sense of connectedness as an individual to the universe as a whole. But in this case, what is at issue is more than just a sense of participation in what is temporally fundamental; it is also a case of graphically sensing what is materially fundamental and one's inevitable dependence upon it. Ordinary matter is made, at the most fundamental level, of quarks and electrons, and even the most complex entities that are part of my being—my brain, for instance—are composed of those quarks and electrons. What is more, all of the matter visible from the Earth is apparently composed of the very same sort of particles (something that might not be true of the notorious "dark matter" that many scientists believe must be invoked to explain gravitational interactions among heavenly bodies). What more powerful impetus to an awareness of participation and the resultant self-transcendence could one possibly require?

Quantum entanglement provides another avenue for sensing my participation in the larger cosmos. Quantum mechanics predicts, and experiments have confirmed, that two electrons can be "entangled" in the sense, for example, that the "spin" of particle "a" will always be in the opposite direction from that of particle "b." What is more, given quantum superposition, neither particle will have a definite spin until it is observed (or until it is acted upon by other natural events so that its superposition of possible states collapses, and it settles into one definite state). This allows for the mysterious action-at-a-distance phenomenon that so troubled Einstein when he contemplated the implications of quantum mechanics. Suppose that two electrons were created in the early universe and that they are entangled. As the universe has expanded, the two electrons have ended up light years apart from one another. The spin of both has been indeterminate from their creation to the present moment. But now we have one of the electrons in the laboratory. By observing it, we collapse the set of possible states of the electron, and we determine its spin. But this means that its sister electron, far off in another corner of the universe, must instantaneously lose its simultaneous possession of a number of possible states: its spin is now determined too, namely, as opposite to the laboratory electron, its sister particle. The fate of the laboratory electron has somehow affected the fate of its entangled partner.

As Michio Kaku observes, all of this means that you may have an electron in your body that is entangled with an electron that is located on the other side of the universe.[4] Hence, you may actually be linked to a distant galaxy in a direct, physical fashion. The payoff here is no New Age mumbo-jumbo. Note, for example, that since information cannot be sent via quantum entanglement, there is no violation of the principle that nothing can travel faster than light. It is simply, once more, a matter of an extraordinarily powerful tool for understanding how we participate in the larger universe, and do so, sometimes, in a surprisingly intimate fashion.

The stars too, as has frequently been remarked, are something in which we can understand ourselves as participating. The heavier elements, including the all-important building-block of life, carbon, were not formed in the earliest universe, but rather in the fusion furnaces of stars. When these stars came to the end of their lives, some of them exploded and seeded space with heavy elements that would subsequently become part of the material for planet formation. It turns out, then, that we are indeed "star-stuff." The carbon in our bodies, the molecular lynchpin of our being, was cooked up in the glistening lights of heaven.

Still another example of how the contemporary scientific worldview supports the cultivation of a sense of participation and self-transcendence is biological evolution. At first blush, Darwinian evolution may seem a strange place in which to seek religious inspiration. After all, conservative Christians have, from the Scopes trial to "Intelligent Design" theories, reviled Darwinian theory as the mortal enemy of piety. But, of course, our interest here is with informed accounts of evolution, not with ideologically blinded versions. And contemplation of the evolution of the species and how it produces *Homo Sapiens* tremendously expands our sense of participation. For now, who I am is not only tied to the fate of the rest of my fellow human beings, but to all of the biological entities that have ever lived upon the earth, since we are all ultimately part of the same evolutionary narrative. Even the evolutionary paths that turned out to be dead ends indirectly affect our being. A dramatic example of how this is so is provided by recognizing that if animals that became extinct had survived instead, *Homo Sapiens*, or at least our progenitors, might have been their prey.

As evolutionary biologist Olivia Judson observes, "Although Mother Nature's infinite variety seems incomprehensible at first, it is not. The forces of nature are not random." Indeed, evolution transforms what would otherwise seem an inchoate grab-bag of living entities "into a magnificent tapestry, a tapestry we can contemplate and begin to understand." In addition to the possibility of participation in this tapestry, Judson finds another existential payoff: "In putting ourselves into our place in nature, in comparing ourselves with other species, we have a real hope of reaching a better understanding, and appreciation, of ourselves."[5]

Piety is a matter of participation and self-transcendence, specifically a participation and self-transcendence in which I focus upon an appropriate object of ultimate concern, something that determines my being and nonbeing. The natural universe surely fits the bill here, given all of the opportunities for the decisive sort of participation and self-transcendence that it affords. As a wholly proper object of ultimate concern, the universe can serve the existential function associated with the word *God*.

Theories of Everything

What of our third topic here, namely, TOEs or "theories of everything"? Physicists since Einstein have sought to unify the four fundamental forces that characterize our universe: gravity; electromagnetism; the strong nuclear force (which binds the nucleus of the atom together); and the weak nuclear force (which is responsible for radioactive decay). This quest for force unification, for a "unified field theory," is connected with the need to reconcile the two most successful theories of twentieth-century physics, Einstein's general theory of relativity (which explains gravity) and quantum mechanics. If we could, indeed, see how all of these forces fit together in a perfect unity, at least back at the time of the Big Bang, then we would in essence have, say many physicists, a theory of everything. In recent decades, there has been an unprecedented flurry of activity in the quest for a successful unification theory, and there are tantalizing suggestions that such a theory might be within our reach (though the question of how such highly abstract and mathematically generated theories could receive experimental support or be experimentally falsified is a continual sticking point). The two leading candidates for such an epochal theory are currently string theory (with its offshoot, "brane" or "membrane" theory) and the theory of loop quantum gravity (the latter is focused specifically upon reconciling general relativity and quantum mechanics but also holds out the prospect of complete force unification).[6]

What might a TOE do for the spiritual quest? Stephen Hawking has, of course, famously said that "if we do discover a complete theory . . . we would know the mind of God."[7] Hawking's God-talk, however, turns out to be a mere poetic flourish. As the late Carl Sagan wrote in his Introduction to Hawking's best-known book, Hawking's position actually suggests "the absence of God," at least when God is taken as the self-conscious creator of the universe.[8] But surely, at least from the perspective of radical theology and radical spirituality, a TOE has much to offer, for a sense of the oneness of the universe—what we referred to in chapter four as the "material" oneness, both cognitive and ontological, of the universe—is a prerequisite for the most profound form of participation and self-transcendence.

Perhaps our sense of the *tremendum* is further enhanced by the possibility that the *ultimate* oneness of reality, if there be such, is not a oneness that characterizes our own universe but, rather, that holds together a multiverse, an ever-unfolding multiplicity of universes. Each universe may have its own set of unifying laws and constants. To contemplate the fact that we may have the opportunity to participate in more than one universe—in the sense, for example, that the gravitational force that holds us upon the Earth may also reach out into other dimensions of space and time (hence explaining its weakness relative to the other fundamental forces)—is surely to be struck with the awe of which Rudolf Otto so eloquently speaks in his description of the sacred.[9]

Our appreciation for the place of the oneness of reality in the spiritual quest can be enhanced by stepping back and glancing at the history of Western philosophy. The Hellenistic philosophers—Plotinus, for example—often championed the notion of the One as a candidate for ultimate reality. Anything with parts is subject to decay and dissipation: it can come "a-part." Every finite reality is composite. It is composed of parts and thus will eventually come undone. Only the wholly simple, the radically One, is without parts and hence beyond dissipation. The One is eternal. And as the simple source of the non-simple or composite entities that make up our world, the One can be identified with Being. As such, it is the worthiest object of the spiritual quest.

As is well known, early Christian thinkers were hardly immune to the lure of Greek philosophy, however disturbing that fact may be to Protestant historians of doctrine such as Adolf von Harnack. Arguably the greatest thinker in the history of Christian theology, Thomas Aquinas affirmed the divine simplicity and identified God with *esse*, the pure act of being. For Aquinas, God's essence is equivalent to his existence. And in the twentieth century, Paul Tillich equated God with "being-itself." Indeed, as we noted in an earlier chapter, Christian thinkers through the ages have sometimes gone so far as to interpret the divine name "I Am," revealed to Moses, as suggesting the identification of God with Being (Exod. 3:14).

The notion that the One, or pure undivided Being, should be the aim-point of the spiritual quest is not difficult to understand. The search for meaning is a search for orientation, for a sense of exactly what my purpose is in the world. If there are many different candidates for the source of meaning and purpose, then we are left not with a happy abundance but, on the contrary, with an anxiety-producing lack of direction. Which source is the right one, and how can I possibly find out? Just in practical spiritual terms, one of the great steps forward represented by the introduction of Jewish monotheism is that it provided a single unambiguous source of meaning and purpose for the devotees of Yahweh. Oneness means direction, certainty, and peace for the soul.[10] Hence, it is that a theory of everything, which would provide a picture of the physical universe in its essential unity, could be a powerful object of participation and self-transcendence.

Attending Reality

The whole spiritual project of participation and self-transcendence surely requires a special sort of attunement. To genuinely participate in a reality beyond myself, in the sense required for spiritual growth and self-overcoming, seems to demand something akin to what the Buddhist tradition calls "mindfulness." In our discussion above of the transforming Zen attitude toward a mountain, we have already had occasion to tap Buddhism's penchant for disciplining and even transforming consciousness of our world. The concept of mindfulness provides a particularly clear window upon this aspect of Buddhism.

For a lucid application of Buddhist mindfulness to the world revealed by science, we look to an essay titled "Mindful Virtue, Mindful Reverence," by cell biologist Ursula Goodenough (whom we met in chapter three) and moral philosopher Paul Woodruff.[11] For these authors, "Mindfulness is knowledge or wisdom that pulls the whole mind and heart of the knower toward a connection with the way things are in all their exciting particularity."[12] The sense of cognitive participation is palpable here:

> Mindfulness is both a state of mind and a practice. The practice, popularized in the West by the Vietnamese Zen master Thich Nhat Hanh, is summarized by his famous epigram "Washing the Dishes to Wash the Dishes." That is, one trains oneself to keep one's consciousness alive to the present reality, to focus attention on the here and now, on the miracle of soap and water and the dishes and the process, rather than rushing through the chore mindlessly to get to whatever is next. In his sutra on Mindfulness, the Buddha refers to mindfulness as one of the enlightenment factors, along with others such as joy,

tranquility, concentration, and equanimity. The mindful
person, Buddhism tells us, assumes the attitude of pure
observation, freed from all false views, and apprehends a
reality that is not only objective but also becomes subjective. The mindful person really sees.[13]

What is more, mindfulness encompasses not only participation in
the world about us, but also self-transcendence:

> Mindfulness entails an immersion, a personal appropria-
> tion of reality. Aristotle describes it as a complex response
> of the entire personality; Nhat Hahn writes that when
> we practice mindfulness of objects outside ourselves,
> the knowledge of these objects becomes mind; and the
> Confucians tell us that we must attain a deep personal
> understanding of our own being and the being of oth-
> ers if we are to respond faithfully to their reality. What is
> sought, they explain, is *self-transformation through a per-
> sonal grasp.*[14]

But how does the practice of mindfulness relate specifically to natural science? "Scientists," say Goodenough and Woodruff, "trained
in a particular kind of 'pure observation,' have provisioned us with
stunning understandings of the natural world," and these understandings then provide "countless substrates for mindful apprehen-
sion." Biology alone, for instance, calls us to be

- mindful of our place in the scheme of things
- mindful that life evolved, that humans are primates
- mindful of the dynamics of molecular life and its emergent
  properties
- mindful of the fragility of life and its ecosystems
- mindful that life and the planet are wildly improbable
- mindful that all of life is interconnected
- mindful of the uniqueness of each creature
- mindful of future generations[15]

Again, physicist Brian Greene reports on how Richard Feyn-
man, one of the most important scientific minds of the twentieth

century, "explained how he could experience the fragrance and beauty of the flower as fully as anyone, but how his knowledge of physics enriched the experience enormously because he could also take in the wonder and magnificence of the underlying molecular, atomic, and subatomic processes."[16] In a whole host of ways, then, contemporary natural science provides invaluable resources for the radical religious quest.

CHAPTER SIX

Science Does Not Need Radical Theology, But . . .

Natural science is an independent enterprise—indeed, the more independent the better: Science can only approach the goal of showing us the world as it is in itself if scientific investigation is not skewed by ideological certitudes or personal existential obsessions. Theology, radical or otherwise, must never be allowed to worm its way into the actual practice of scientific theorizing and investigation. But that is not to say that there might not be advantages to *appending* theological insights to what science accomplishes all by itself. A strong, eloquent case for the need to unify our scientific vision of the cosmos with the "more" provided by theology is made by our sometime guide from chapter one, Nancey Murphy. In *The Moral Nature of the Universe: Theology, Cosmology, and Ethics*, Murphy and co-author George Ellis contend that the scientific worldview ought to be completed by both ethical and metaphysical-theological principles.[1] Of course, Murphy and Ellis have in mind a more traditional theological vision than the one for which I have been contending in this book. But we can nonetheless follow their lead by thinking about the relationship of science to ethics and to metaphysics and theology.

Science Needs Ethics

The claim that science should be completed by an ethical vision is, in a sense, the easy argument to be made here. Science, of course, has its own internal procedural principles that already have more than a patina of ethical substance. One must bracket one's prejudices and predilections in setting up one's experiments. One must formulate one's theories and gather one's data in a spirit as free of personal prejudices and predilections as possible. I might *want* to be the first scientist to discover how to effect cold-water fusion, but I need to hold back my selfish desire for fame and Nobel-Prize-fortune if I am to view the data objectively and allow the world to speak. And I must be fully open to the efforts of others to test my reported results. It is when we move beyond "pure" science to the technological spin-offs of scientific research that extra-scientific ethical principles become an issue. It is an easy argument that technological research and production should be informed by independent moral principles because contemporary technology can have such incredibly far-reaching effects, for good and for ill, upon the earth and the human race. One need think only about contemporary weapons research and production (including the burgeoning interest in space-based weapons) and genetic research and manipulation for evidence here.

It should be apparent that many different ethical perspectives could fruitfully be brought to bear upon contemporary scientific technology and used to guide the technological enterprise. There is no *prima facie* reason for supposing that the requisite ethical framework must be a theologically generated one. My argument here is simply that the pattern of participation and self-transcendence to which we have nailed our theological flag is a useful generator of ethical guidelines. The notion of participation in nature probably applies most directly to the sort of ethical principles already implicit in the endeavor of "pure" science: I attempt actually to enter into the reality outside myself so that I can grasp it as it is in and of itself. But the notion of participation *and self-transcendence* is directly applicable to the issue of technology and its uses. While I am not an ethicist, and it is not my intention to propose a specific set of ethical guidelines here, it should be evident that a notion of collective self-transcendence—as a nation and as a species—can provide a powerful starting point for the ethical regulation of our use of technology. I am not the center of the universe, nor is the whole species Homo Sapiens. Hence only those technologies are ethically justified that avoid irreparable harm to my fellow human beings and the larger physical universe. We are fully capable of constructing land mines that spew shrapnel in a fashion that intentionally maims the mine victims, demoralizing them and terrorizing their comrades in arms as well as the local citizenry. But the principle of self-transcendence clearly suggests that the mere fact that we *can* make such weapons does not mean that we *should* make them.

Science Needs an Ultimate Framework

The more difficult argument to make is that science needs not only ethical augmentation but also some sort of wider explanatory matrix into which it can be fit and that that matrix should be supplied by radical theology. That this need exists is by no means immediately apparent. Let us explore this issue in four stages. First, one might argue that NASA's Mars rovers, Spirit and Opportunity, "did science" on the red planet. In that case, pure science hardly needs some larger meaning-framework: a machine can do it. Of course, the rovers were programmed and overseen by a bevy of very human scientists here on earth. The machines were not really doing science by themselves.

Second, we must take note of the fact that, just as science has a modicum of ethical principles built into its very methods, human scientists seem automatically to bring some larger framework of meaning to their work. After all, one chooses to engage in scientific research for a reason, and at least where good scientists are concerned, that reason will not simply be to earn a living. Rather, scientific research satisfies the basic human trait that we call curiosity. What is more, those engaged in cutting-edge scientific research frequently experience a sense of intellectual delight and even, perhaps, a sense of wonder. Science may even, all by itself, have implications for that most basic question: the very meaning of human life. Brian Greene insists that "Assessing existence while failing to embrace the insights of modern physics would be like wrestling in the dark with an unknown opponent. By deepening our understanding of the true nature of physical reality, we profoundly reconfigure our sense of ourselves and our experience of the universe."[2] Thus, scientific work, as it is actually carried out by human beings, seems automatically to bring with it a potent existential component. It is not a matter of following rote procedures bereft of human significance. On one level, then, science appears to need no help from theology to generate humanly significant meaning.

It is when we move to the third stage of our analysis that the case can be made for a theological contribution to science. Perhaps the intellectual delight and wonder that often accompany science by the very nature of scientific inquiry are still not enough. Ultimately, is it not desirable that major components of our relation to reality—intellectual-scientific, ethical, aesthetic, and spiritual, for example—all fit together into a harmonious worldview? Surely, having a compartmentalized, schizoid approach to reality is not the most productive of arrangements.

Now Murphy and Ellis contend that science *must*, in the sense of an intellectual imperative, be completed by metaphysics and theology. For them, there are various boundary questions that go beyond scientific competence. These are questions to which science points, but which, given its very nature, it cannot answer. For example, Murphy and Ellis claim that science cannot explain why our universe has the particular laws that it does, and they connect this issue with the familiar anthropic argument about the apparent fine-tuning of the universe for life mentioned in chapter four above.[3] But this is a dangerous line of argument, in that, as we saw in chapter one, theorists such as Brian Greene hypothesize that a successful unified field theory might well make it clear that the particular laws that our universe displays are the only laws that it could have displayed.

Furthermore, Murphy and Ellis (along with other contemporary theists[4]) put forth a "kenotic" interpretation of God's action and of the human ethic that they believe it implies. The concept of kenosis, a Greek term that means literally "self-emptying," is found in Paul's letter to the Philippians where he explains how God humbly engages in kenosis in taking on flesh in Jesus of Nazareth

(Phil. 2:5-8). For Murphy and Ellis, this kenotic approach applies to all of God's dealings with his creation, as well as to how we should live: "God appears to work in concert with nature, never overriding or violating the very processes that God has created."[5] But surely this is to invite into the picture a close relative of that most infamous of theological guests, the "God of the gaps." The phrase refers, of course, to the temptation to which many theologians have succumbed since science arrived upon the scene: while science now explains many natural phenomena that we used to explain by invoking God, there are still gaps in scientific knowledge. Thus, we can point to where God is to be found by gesturing to those gaps. The devastating problem with the "God of the gaps" strategy, however, is that science marches on, and the gaps inevitably get closed. The kenotic approach to God does not depend upon specific gaps in our scientific knowledge. But it intentionally hides God amidst natural processes so that we cannot detect any sort of divine intervention that would transgress the laws of nature. One does not have to be an old-fashioned logical positivist to see that a God who acts in a fashion that is invisible when scientists check to make sure that their laws are not violated is a God of existential claims that cannot be falsified. Such a talented Master of Disguise might not be an impotent God, but claims for his existence based on what we see in the cosmos are, for all practical purposes, impotent. And, of course, there is the whole problem that we explored in chapter one: attempts to construe the doctrine of God in such a way that God could both kenotically hide—he does not violate energy conservation, for example—and yet still affect the world appear, at least thus far, to fail. The pantheistic God does not supernaturally intervene in nature either, but, of course, the pantheistic God is not defined by the claim that it can do so.

Theology Integrating the Scientific Quest

A scientifically informed pantheism based upon the dynamic of participation and self-transcendence can, I contend, do a much better job of providing an overarching framework that unifies the scientific worldview and our larger existential concerns. First of all, it is apparent that "God" as the whole of the cosmos in its role as the focus of our ultimate concern does not in any fashion violate the canons of contemporary science. But, of course, this merely negative coherence, this noninterference, is not good enough. There must be a positive, content-rich coherence. We can find this positive coherence by thinking back to the previous chapter. That is, the way in which radical theology and spirituality can benefit from science is the key, reciprocally, to how radical spirituality can take the scientific worldview up into a meaningful human whole, thereby benefiting science. Our radical theology finds vast spiritual resources in the world revealed by natural science, for it is a world that invites participation and self-transcendence. I sense my participation in the whole dynamic that begins in the Big Bang, moves through nucleo-synthesis in the stars, and provides for the evolution of life on earth. With the aid of techniques such as Buddhist mindfulness, I can participate in a self-overcoming fashion in everything from the starry heavens to the mountains that rise out of the earth's crust. Furthermore, those individual objects that science opens for my participation, such as a mountain, can in turn stand in for the universe as a whole, in which I can then participate

That is what science does for radical piety. But, to the extent that such participation and self-overcoming fit seamlessly with the scientific worldview, indeed can be drawn out of that worldview (among other dimensions of human experience), it is quite possible to reverse the arrow. Science just in and of itself, as an intellectual inquiry about nature, needs no enhancement or additions; it is already complete. But as a human activity that one wishes to mesh with one's larger outlook on human existence, it can profitably be taken up into the spiritual project of participation and self-transcendence and seen as one crucial instance of that project.

The God involved here is by no means in hiding: He/She is the Whole to which all objects of participation, including those so helpfully uncovered by science, point. And the larger framework into which science is taken up here is not a metaphysical one, but, rather, a pragmatic existential framework. That is, this framework does not involve any truth claims that could end up contradicting scientific discoveries, such as the possible discovery that a successful unified field theory reveals how the laws of physics in our universe could not have been otherwise.[6] In summary, then, science in itself does not need radical theology in this scenario, but an individual human being who does science, or even who simply appropriates the scientific worldview, can find in radical theology the resources for integrating science into her or his larger existential worldview.

Technology, Theology, and the Future

But there is also a fourth level to consider: it has to do with what may well turn out to be the most important scientific technology of the future. But here our interest lies not in the aforementioned ethical ramifications of technology, but, rather, in how this technology will redefine what it means to be human, and in how well prepared theology is to deal with that redefinition. My focus is the controversial yet ever-advancing field of so-called "artificial intelligence," or "AI," and related endeavors. Allow me to bring some degree of order to the case I wish to make by distinguishing three discreet steps that I believe will inevitably be taken in the development of human-made minds. First, computer scientists are, as the notion of AI suggests, struggling to develop *thinking* machines. Second, machines will one day become *self-conscious* thinking things. And third, those self-conscious artificial entities will eventually become *moral and spiritual agents*. We begin, then, with intelligent machines. Ray Kurzweil, the computer scientist and theorist who authored *The Age of Intelligent Machines*, opines in his later book, *The Age of Spiritual Machines*, that intelligence can be defined as "the ability to use optimally limited resources—including time—to achieve . . . [specified] goals."[7] In Kurzweil's view, there are already plenty of promising strategies being tested, and they will lead to genuinely intelligent machines in the near future. By some definitions of intelligence, we may already possess intelligent machines. In 1997, IBM's Deep Blue defeated chess master Gary Kasparov. Deep Blue had the ability to consider the outcomes of a whole host of possible moves on the chessboard, and it chose those moves best suited to counter Kasparov's play. In some respects, at least, Deep Blue must certainly be considered an intelligent machine.

Can machines ever take the next step and become self-conscious? That is a much greater challenge than mere intelligence. After all, scientists and philosophers have yet to unravel the secrets of our own human self-consciousness. How does the physical entity we call the brain produce something that seems so non-physical? It is not surprising that David Chalmers has dubbed consciousness, especially in the guise of "experience," as the "hard problem" in philosophy of mind.[8] But progress is steadily being made, progress that will most likely make it possible not only to understand the nature of human self-consciousness but to construct machines in which self-consciousness emerges. Neuro-philosopher Dan Lloyd, for example, has creatively meshed Husserlian phenomenology, which shows how important time-awareness is in our experience of self-consciousness, with contemporary neuroscience and its latest brain scanning technologies. Our "retention" of the immediate past of a phenomenon and our "protension" of how the phenomenon will unfold in the immediate future, melded with the present moment, is a lynchpin of our self-conscious awareness of the world. Lloyd offers provocative suggestions about how such crucial time-consciousness might be replicated in technologies such as neural nets.[9]

Of course, there is an almost instinctual suspicion of the notion that our self-consciousness is purely a function of that physical organ we call the brain. But a very simple and straightforward example can be adduced to buttress the contention that mind and brain are indeed one. Let us call it, rather inelegantly, the "mean drunk" example. Human beings have been imbibing alcohol and similar substances for a significant part of their history. It cannot be denied that the purely physical changes effected in brain chemistry by alcohol can result in changes in consciousness, from euphoria to a distortion of our perception of space. But this effect of a chemical substance upon consciousness goes further than simply affecting feelings and senses: it can, in a very real sense, affect who we are. Enter the mean drunk, that all-too-familiar character who is a relatively stable human being when sober, but who becomes a wife beater and a child beater when drunk. What is crucial to note here is that beating one's wife and children is not akin to alcohol altering one's reaction-time. Rather, it has to do with one's sense of *moral* responsibilities, and it affects one's *moral* choices. What could be closer to our identity, or even to what some might wish to call the "soul"?

The upshot is that the mind, or even the "soul," is a function of the brain, which suggests that science *will* someday be able to offer a complete analysis of the mechanisms of consciousness, and we *will* be able to reproduce those mechanisms within an artificial brain—what could be logically impossible about doing so? Of course, we shall never be able cognitively to crawl within the machine and feel its self-consciousness. For that reason, we will never be absolutely certain that the artificial brain is self-conscious, just as we can never be absolutely certain that other human beings are conscious in the way that we are (though there is, one presumes, a stronger argument from analogy in the case of other humans). Hence, I am in sympathy with Kurzweil when he asks, "What possible experiment can we run that would conclusively prove whether an entity or process is conscious?"[10] But I also agree that "machines will convince us that they are conscious, that they have their own agenda worthy of our respect. We will come to believe they are conscious much as we believe that of each other."[11]

Kurzweil's use of the word *respect* in the quotation immediately above takes us to the third step of my argument, to the claim that machines will become moral and spiritual agents. For that is what happens in our own case: once we are fully self-conscious, and given our ability to think and judge (components of the first step, namely, intelligence), we experience ourselves as responsible moral agents as well as agents able to take a stance on matters of meaning and self-transcendence. Of course, moral and spiritual agency presupposes *freedom*, and that is perhaps a more difficult phenomenon to understand than even self-consciousness! If self-consciousness is exhaustively explicable in terms of scientifically available processes within the brain, along with the brain's interaction with its environment (being-in-the-world), how can we genuinely be free? The brain's electro-chemical symphony, after all, presumably obeys all of the laws of physics and chemistry, which suggests, in turn, that everything that the brain produces, including our self-consciousness and our decisions, are fully determined. Many physicists and philosophers will conclude that this is the end of the story: freedom is an illusion. Much as Spinoza's rock falling in a gravitational field supposes itself to be free out of mere ignorance of the causal network in which it is enmeshed, so our own ignorance is a precondition of our experience of being free. Other theorists offer a bit more optimistic picture, however. Physicist Roger Penrose, for example, has famously suggested that quantum indeterminacy might bubble up into brain processes with sufficient potency to allow for human freedom.[12] Yet, indeterminacy by itself cannot be the answer, for free choice is hardly equivalent to a completely undetermined, arbitrary decision. There must be a strong element of purposefulness.

For the purposes of my argument here, I am simply going to assume the freedom of the will necessary for moral and spiritual agency. Why? Because Christian theists will do so, and the gist of the argument that I am developing here will turn out to be that a pantheistic radical theology is in a better position to deal with a future filled with electronic agents than is traditional theism.[13] That is, if my argument is with traditional theism, then it is perfectly legitimate for me to accept assumptions embraced by traditional theism itself.

The Changing Human Identity

Just as scientific technology will, in the future, result in self-conscious electronic moral agents, so it will effect vast changes in the nature of *Homo Sapiens*. Not only will scientific technology inevitably produce ever-more-efficient artificial limbs and organs, and replacement organs grown in the laboratory, but it will allow us to augment our brains, and thus our consciousnesses, in extraordinary ways. Surgeons will, for example, be able to implant advanced electronic neural nets into the human brain to significantly augment capacities such as memory, perception, and reasoning.[14] And here is the $64,000 question: will I still be the same person, will I retain the same *identity*, if I undergo such radical alterations to my natural brain functions?

The identity question comes up in another fashion here. Scientific technology has already, for many years now, been extending human life expectancy. Suppose that someday, however far in the future, the average life expectancy for a human being is approximately five hundred years. In the present day and age, where life expectancy averages around seventy-five years in the developed world, continuity of identity is fairly easy to maintain, despite the many new experiences that the world brings my way during my lifetime. In other words, I will experience many identity-augmenting events in my lifetime, perhaps even tragic events such as the loss of loved ones. Each of these experiences undoubtedly changes me in some small way. But the changes are, indeed, sufficiently small that, even in aggregate, they do not so fundamentally change who I am that I have a genuinely different identity at age seventy-five than I had at age ten. But now suppose that I live for five hundred years. The small changes will now be so many that their compilation will perhaps have a decided capacity to change who I am: there will be a very real possibility that I will not maintain identity-in-difference over the course of a lifetime, but that I will be a genuinely different person at age 459 than I was at age ten. The phenomenon that can easily be foreseen here is one that can be labeled "serial identities." Allow me to provide a simplistic example. Fritz will develop a particular identity, given the nature of his genetic heritage, his general environment, and his particular life experiences, an identity that will be relatively stable from zero to one hundred years of age. But there will always be some drift, some free-play in his identity, for identity is always a matter of identity-in-difference. After more than a hundred years of life, Fritz's many different experiences will, in aggregate, so change who he is that we will have to conclude that he no longer possesses the same identity that he had in roughly his first century of existence. And this process of identity drift will go on throughout Fritz's approximately five hundred years of life.

But human beings desire a stable sense of meaning and recognizable centers of gravity around which a sense of identity can orbit. Hence, Fritz will not go through life in a continually amorphous process of identity-drift. That would be to have no identity at all. Rather, at various points in his life, Fritz will re-narrate who he is. Indeed, in order to obtain something like a stable sense of who he is in his different centuries of life (my choice of the century as the touchstone here is, of course, a purely arbitrary one used for purposes of simplification), Fritz will probably have to consciously and deliberately re-narrate his identity. This process might well be accompanied and enabled by formal rites of passage, perhaps decidedly religious and spiritual in nature, wherein Fritz concretizes his latest sense of who he is via appropriating particular symbols and memories. Thus, he will not pass through life with nothing but chaotically shifting experiences, but will develop different nodes of identity, different formally enacted narrations of who he is that rise up at specific junctures in his five-hundred-year life journey.

What we foresee, then, is multiple identities through time for human beings, however far off in the future. And the same will certainly be true for our electronic alter egos. For the self-conscious moral agents that we will build and program (and that will someday build and program their own, electronic kind) can always be radically re-programmed. In the case of our electronic friends, then, we may speak of "serial, re-programmable identities."

Implications for Theology

What does all of this—the creation of machines as moral and spiritual agents with flexible identities and the augmentation of human beings (both via implants and via life-span extension) so that they may lose a singular definitive identity—have to do with theology? We must begin with traditional theism. In the theistic worldview, the essence of who I am, the heart of my identity, is determined by who I am in the mind of God. In a sense, *all* things find their essence just in how they are conceived in the divine intellect, a theistic adaptation of the Platonic philosophy of the Forms that finds clear expression, for example, in Anselm's eleventh-century treatise "Concerning Truth."[15] But human identity and selfhood are particularly guarded by the divine mind. Jesus promises that God counts even the hairs of the individual's head (Matt. 10:30).[16] And this God-origin of the self is also very much the source of the self's dignity. We are children of God, created in God's image (Gen. 1:26). The soul and its worth, then, are clearly God-given in traditional Christian theology.

The fact that my identity, the essence of who I am, resides in the divine intention, for me, is what makes sin so tragic on the individual level (sin also having devastating social consequences, of course). For sin is rebellion against God and thus leads to my estrangement from God. But if I am estranged from God, then I am estranged from my very self and will never come to the fulfillment intended by God. Hence, Augustine's famous prayer, "Thou hast formed us for Thyself, and our hearts are restless until they find rest in Thee."[17] And hence, the Kierkegaardian contention that we become who we are only by standing before God.

But the machines of the future, self-conscious moral and spiritual agents though they will be, will not be created by God, but by human beings. These machines will have identities, but not identities held fast in the divine mind. They will be yet another step removed from God when they reproduce, that is, when intelligent, self-conscious machines begin to design and build other intelligent, self-conscious machines. Yet these machine-produced machines will have identities and dignity too. They will be moral and spiritual agents. And the situation only becomes more provocative when we realize that we might wish radically to alter the identity of a machine. The altered product would still be a self-conscious agent, but it would have a wholly new identity.

And what about the alterations of ourselves mentioned above? What happens to the notion that I am who I am based on who I am meant to be by God, when I can change crucial aspects of my identity through technological augmentation, or when my identity changes altogether according to the pattern of serial identities?

We gain two insights from these considerations, I think, both radical. First, what makes someone or some thing a self-conscious moral and spiritual agent worthy of our respect—worthy to be treated always as an end, never as a means, as Immanuel Kant would say—is not a function of its having a specific identity and telos hidden in the divine mind. For *Homo Sapiens* will soon be able to make such beings; we will have the ability to alter these machines' identities whenever it is fitting, so that they can be said to have serial, re-programmable identities; electronic moral agents will at some point learn to reproduce *themselves*; and human beings will someday adopt serial identities, both through electronic augmentation and through centuries-long life spans. Some new theology, other than the traditional perspective according to which the identity and dignity of moral and spiritual agents are given by their being planned for and held fast in the divine consciousness, will need to be developed to take account of the facts of the being of moral and spiritual agents. It will no longer make sense to say, with the Apostle Paul, "God . . . set me apart before I was born and called me through his grace" (Gal. 1:15).

Second, the notion of a stable, "centered" identity itself seems to come under attack here. That there is something akin to the form of my identity in the mind of God that makes me who I am makes no sense if, even apart from sin, I can have no single, life-long identity. The self needs to be understood as akin to the mere construction described by David Hume back in the eighteenth century, or as the "de-centered" self of much post-modern theorizing, a self held together by the narrative that we concoct (though the fact that we have arrived at this notion of de-centering via a consideration of technology rather than from post-modern philosophizing means that we are in no way committed to any of the other tenets of postmodernism, especially those that call into question the power of science).

It turns out, however, that our scientifically informed pantheism can handle the challenge before us with aplomb. What forms the deepest spiritual dimensions of Fritz's identity, beyond, or perhaps in conjunction with, whatever rites of passage he undergoes in the history of his serial identities? His spiritual identity will be formed by his unique location, at a given point in his multiform biography, in the web of participation and self-transcendence. Recalling and continually refreshing that participation will be the way in which Fritz becomes the particular person that he is. The notion that the ultimate form of such participation and self-transcendence manifests itself in participation in the universe revealed by science is just as workable in this imagined future as it is in our actual present.

In summary of this chapter, then, we have concluded, first, that while science qua science needs no advice from theology, theology has a contribution to make in several areas. First, theology, including radical theology, can provide ethical guidelines for the creation and use of scientific technologies. Second, while I disagree with Murphy and Ellis that science necessarily points to certain theological-metaphysical tenets, I have attempted to show that a radical theology can provide an optional unifying framework that handily integrates the insights of natural science into one's larger sense of self and reality. Finally, an analysis of the relationship of theology to scientific technologies should be proactive, anticipating the technologies of the future. On this particular matter, I have suggested that a scientifically informed pantheism can deal with profound questions of identity that will arise as scientific technologies progress, questions that traditional theism appears not to have the resources to answer.

CHAPTER SEVEN

Radical Prospects

What, then, are the prospects for a fusion of radical theology and science? What are its weaknesses and its strengths? The United States is, of course, a peculiarly pious nation. Over 90 percent of poll respondents consistently report that they believe in God. Perhaps not all of those answering the God-question think of God in terms of the transcendent personal consciousness of traditional biblical theism, but no doubt the majority do. For most Americans, then, it may well be that the radical theology and its merger with science proposed in these pages is a nonstarter. The y will simply be uninterested in a God that seems but a shadow of the God in which they believe. Perhaps, they are only interested, for example, in a God that can provide them with personal immortality, something that the pantheistic deity clearly cannot do.

But let us take care not to limit our vision overly much. What about that vast majority of scientists in the prestigious National Academy of Sciences, cited earlier, who say that they do not believe in God? Might not at least some of them find the God presented in these pages attractive? And what happens when we leave U.S. shores? The United States is unusually religious, opine many sociologists, because the lack of any established church in our history and the resultant religious pluralism have resulted in an environment characterized by religious competition and marketing. It is this competition and vigorous marketing that have kept the churches alive in America. But the lives of a very significant proportion of Britons seem to be little affected by belief in the God of traditional Christian theism, or at least by its traditional institutional incarnation. One survey found, a few years ago, that more Britons were watching reruns of *Star Trek* each week than going to church. Traditional piety in France is even harder to find. And when we move to the Scandinavian countries, it is essentially nonexistent. In short, the other post-industrial societies in the world simply do not have the investment in the God of biblical theism that Americans seem to have.[1] But these societies are surely invested in the scientific worldview, and to the extent that their citizens desire *some* sort of spirituality, the scientifically informed radical theology that I have worked out in previous chapters cannot be ruled out as an attractive worldview for such persons. Of course, there are persons in our world today who are simply so decidedly secular that they will not be interested in any sort of God-talk whatsoever, however radical and however science-friendly.

But an evaluation of the prospects for the sort of radical theology presented in this book cannot be based simply on the question of how many adherents it is likely to attract. We must also ask how many theoretical problems it solves. In other words, if one wishes to hold onto a life focused upon spirituality and, at the same time, fully to embrace the scientific worldview, how well does the proposed radical approach do in achieving these goals? I have argued, and attempted to show in detail, that the radical approach is, in fact, far superior to traditional theistic approaches to science on such crucial matters as the law of the conservation of energy. If there be any truth to this contention, then the radical theological approach to theology must be deemed to be in a strong position indeed.

One way in which to focus the challenge faced by the proposal made here is to confront it with Daniel Dennett's notion of "belief in belief."[2] Some persons believe in the specific tenets of traditional Christian (or Jewish or Muslim) theism and, if asked, could give a reasonably articulate defense of those tenets. But many others have difficulties with traditional theism's tenets. Yet they are still believers of a sort: they believe in belief. That is, even though they cannot genuinely affirm the specific claims attached to traditional belief in God, they believe that religion and devotion to God is a good thing. Thus, they affirm traditional theism without being able to articulate specific theistic claims to which they can adhere.

One particular phenomenon that Dennett singles out as a candidate for belief in belief is that process in which religious persons
hold onto the term *God*, originally associated in the Abrahamic
religions with the decidedly anthropomorphic protagonist of the
Hebrew Bible, and apply it to something immeasurably more
abstract. Before the enlightenment brought by contemporary biology, natural philosophers used to talk about a "life force," an "*élan
vital*," that supposedly explained the mysterious phenomenon of
life. Today we don't need the concept of the life force. Its work is
done by our understanding of biological phenomena such as DNA.
But wouldn't it be odd, as Dennett points out, if we were to hold
onto the term *life force* and claim that science has now identified
it, that it is DNA? But, for Dennett, this strange practice is exactly
what is at issue in using the anthropomorphic notion of God
found in the Hebrew Bible and linking it with something such as
a radically transcendent, infinite, and omniscient reality beyond
our understanding. This must, he thinks, be an instance of belief
in belief, of being so convinced of the benefits of believing in God
that one continues to support it even when what one really ends up
with would be unrecognizable to the first theists.

How might Dennett's observations about belief in belief apply
to the scientifically informed pantheism that I have attempted to
articulate? Two responses should be made. First, I have given the
pantheism at issue very specific tenets. It is not a matter of belief in
the general benefits of belief, but, rather, of belief in these specific
ideas and goals. Dennett holds—and he is undeniably correct—that
many persons who are asked to define *spirituality* cannot really do so.
Hence, the very claim that the religious or spiritual quest is worthwhile becomes too ambiguous to decode. But, again, the notion
of spirituality with which we have been working has been clearly
defined: it is a matter of participation and self-transcendence, specifically, a participation and self-transcendence worthy of our ultimate concern in that it aids us in living productively in the face of
the slings and arrows of finitude, such as death, moral inadequacy,
and meaninglessness.

Second, I have mentioned, at least in passing, specific reasons for continuing to utilize God-talk in referring to the project

envisioned here. For instance, in the discussion of Sallie McFague's work, I pointed out how important it is to have access to the notion of God *as a symbol*, in order to provide a concrete object of consciousness. Such concreteness is necessary for ultimate concern, a focal point around which to see all of life. Furthermore, genuine dedication to a life of attunement to the cosmos, in such a way that the cosmos can be crucial to one's ultimate concern, requires something akin to the traditional religious rituals and disciplines through which devotees have always oriented their lives to what they conceived as ultimate. To the extent that these rituals and disciplines are tied up with God-talk, we have another reason for preserving the use of the term *God*, and even the idea of God.

Of course, even if one grants that the pantheism presented here is not an example of belief in belief and recognizes it as a clear and substantive proposal, that does not mean that she or he will have to find this pantheism attractive. This pantheism makes no claims at all about the existence of supernatural or occult entities. The decision to embrace it is perhaps, in the end, more akin to self-consciously and actively enjoying music than it is to affirming traditional belief in God. The difference between a person who makes enjoying music one of his most significant hobbies and one who is largely uninterested in music is not a difference of belief in the ordinary sense. There is no contention over whether music exists. Rather, it is all a matter of preference. One person enjoys music, while the other is indifferent. Is the person who actively pursues music, who builds up a CD collection or ipod playlist running the gamut from Handel to Hindemith to Hendrix, better off then the one who is tone deaf? In some ways, we might argue that the music lover is, indeed, better off. After all, music appears to enrich human experience and to produce an impressive amount of joy. But, of course, the tone deaf or indifferent person in our example may have a hobby that the music lover does not—bird-watching, for example, or backyard astronomy, or following NASCAR racing—that produces as much enrichment and joy as music does for the music lover.

But is not our pantheism superior to bird-watching and the enjoyment of music and NASCAR, in that it is inextricably connected with self-transcendence and, hence, with a degree of moral sensitivity? Perhaps so. But while committing to pantheism may be more important than embracing hobbies, one clearly does not have to embrace a scientifically informed pantheism in order to experience self-transcendence or to be moral. One can experience self-transcendence and be moral by traveling some completely different route.

It seems, then, that we are left with the policy of "different strokes for different folks." We can take our cue from the Indian religious tradition here, specifically from the Bagavahd Gita: different paths to insight, different yogic journeys, are available to different kinds of persons. Some people are more attuned to the intellect, and some, to action, the emotions, or meditative experiences. There is a path for each. Let a thousand flowers bloom. A scientifically informed pantheism, such as the one sketched here, makes a great deal of sense for people of a certain disposition, or so I would argue. It does not describe a way of life that all must embrace, or that the rejection of which results in devastating spiritual impoverishment.

In the end, however, we must come full circle back to the central point made in the Preface: the radical position, at least if it is reasonably well articulated, deserves to be heard just insofar as *all* serious voices ought to be included in the dialogue between religion and science. We are on a quest, both spiritual and intellectual. As such, we should welcome whatever voices can aid us in better understanding the nature of that quest and in walking its difficult way.

NOTES

Introduction

1 A classic example of the conflict view is Andrew Dickson White, *A History of the Warfare of Science with Theology in Christendom* (London and New York: D. Appleton and Company, 1896).

2 The Paul Tillich of *Dynamics of Faith* (New York: Harper and Row, 1957) provides a good example, as we shall see in chapter one, although he believed theology ought to interest itself in the world of nature, as evidenced by the third volume of his *Systematic Theology* (Chicago: University of Chicago, 1963). Karl Rahner, the most important Roman Catholic theologian of the twentieth century, stands in proximity to Tillich. He, too, spends little time analyzing specific scientific issues. Good inheritor of the Thomistic tradition that he is, however, Rahner, of course, has an appreciation for the role of nature and of "natural theology." Some influential Protestant theologians of the period reinforced the separation of science and religion by simply ignoring nature altogether. They held that it is the realm of "history" that counts as far as faith is concerned, for it is within history that God acts and provides for our salvation. The preeminent examples here are Karl Barth and Rudolf Bultmann.

3 See Richard Dawkins, *The God Delusion* (Boston: Houghton Mifflin, 2006). See also Sam Harris, *The End of Faith* (New York: Norton, 2005); and Victor J. Stenger, *God: The Failed Hypothesis* (Amherst, N.Y.: Prometheus, 2007).

4 H. Allen Orr, for example, claims that Dawkins cannot tolerate "the meticulous reasoning of theologians." See "A Mission to Convert," *The New York Review of Books,* January 11, 2007, 22. Novelist Marilynne Robinson implies something similar when she suggests that Dawkins, in his main argument against belief in God, overlooks "an ancient given of theology." See "Hysterical Scientism: The Ecstasy of Richard Dawkins," *Harper's,* November 2006, 86.

5 Francis Ellingwood Abbot, *Scientific Theism* (Boston: Little, Brown, 1885).

6 See, for example, Pierre Teilhard de Chardin, *The Phenomenon of Man* (New York: Harper Torchbooks, 1959).

7 See Ian Barbour, *Religion in an Age of Science: The Gifford Lectures 1989–1991, Volume* 1, (San Francisco: Harper and Row, 1990); Arthur R. Peacocke, "God's Interaction with the World: The Implications of Deterministic 'Chaos' and of Interconnected and Interdependent Complexity," in *Chaos and Complexity: Scientific Perspectives on Divine Action,* ed. Robert John Russell, Nancey Murphy, and Arthur R. Peacocke (Vatican City State: Vatican Observatory Publications, and Berkeley: The Center for Theology and the Natural Sciences, 1995), 263–88; John Polkinghorne, "Chaos and Divine Action," in *Religion and Science: History, Method, Dialogue,* ed. W. Mark Richardson and Wesley J. Wildman (New York: Routledge, 1996), 242–53; and Nancey Murphy, "Divine Action in the Natural Order: Buridan's Ass and Schrödinger's Cat," in *Chaos and Complexity,* 325–58. We shall consider these thinkers in chapter one.

8 "Faith seeking understanding" is the formula representing the Augustinian approach to faith and reason. The phrase itself comes from the all-important eleventh-century theologian Anselm of Canterbury.

CHAPTER 1

1 For reassessments of the old warfare model of the relationship between religion and science in modernity, see, for example, John Hedley Brooke, "Science and Theology in the Enlightenment," in *Religion and Science: History, Method, Dialogue,* ed. W. Mark Richardson and Wesley J. Wildman (New York: Routledge, 1996), 7–27; and Claude Welch, "Dispelling Some Myths About the Split between Theology and Science in the Nineteenth Century," in *Religion and Science,* 29–40.

2 Timothy Ferris, *Coming of Age in the Milky Way* (New York: William Morrow, 1988), 122.

3 N. Max Wildiers, *The Theologian and His Universe: Theology and Cosmology from the Middle Ages to the Present,* trans. Paul Dunphy (New York: Seabury, 1982), 43, 46, 177.

4 See Sharon Begley, "Science Finds God," *Newsweek,* (July 20, 1998, 46–51; George Johnson, "True Believers: Science and Religion Cross Their Line in the Sand," *The New York Times,* July 12, 1998, sec. 4, 1, 18; Gregg Easterbrook, "Study of Relation Between Science, Religion Resurrected," reprinted in *The New Haven Register,* March 17, 1999, A13. Gregg Easterbrook, "The New Convergence," *Wired* (December 2002): 165–169.

5 See W. V. Quine and J. S. Ullian, *The Web of Belief,* 2nd ed. (New York: McGraw-Hill, 1978). Foundationalism is an approach to knowledge that holds that some of our beliefs rest upon indubitable "foundations." For instance, some thinkers have claimed that we have sure foundations in truths that are evident to the senses.

6 While I shall succumb to the common wisdom in abandoning the most naive Enlightenment claims about an absolutely objective science, I shall nonetheless maintain a basically realist position toward natural science and what it tells us about our world. See especially chapters three and five below.

7 Timothy Ferris, *The Whole Shebang: A State-of-the-Universe(s) Report* (New York: Simon and Schuster, 1997), 13.

8 See Ian Barbour, *Religion in an Age of Science: The Gifford* Lectures *1989–1991, Volume 1* (San Francisco: Harper and Row, 1990).

9 See John Polkinghorne, "Chaos Theory and Divine Action," in *Religion and Science*, 245.

10 Panpsychism is the position that suggests that the whole universe is, in some sense, pervaded by consciousness. The Whiteheadian version of this suggestion is not to claim that chairs and trees are conscious, but rather that the fundamental constituents of all objects, fundamental entities that Whitehead terms "actual occasions," possess a rudimentary form of consciousness, in that they can "prehend" or "feel" possibilities presented to them and actualize those possibilities. See Alfred North Whitehead, *Process and Reality: An Essay on Cosmology* (New York: Harper and Row, 1957).

11 Polkinghorne, "Chaos Theory," 247.

12 Polkinghorne, "Chaos Theory," 247 (italics mine).

13 Polkinghorne, "Chaos Theory," 247.

14 Nancey Murphy, "Divine Action in the Natural Order: Buridan's Ass and Schrödinger's Cat," in *Chaos and Complexity: Scientific Perspectives on Divine Action*, ed. Robert John Russell, Nancey Murphy, and Arthur R. Peacocke (Vatican City State: Vatican Observatory Publications, and Berkeley: The Center for Theology and the Natural Sciences, 1995), 327.

15 Murphy, "Divine Action in the Natural Order," 328.

16 See Arthur R. Peacocke, "God's Interaction with the World: The Implications of Deterministic 'Chaos' and of Interconnected and Interdependent Complexity," in *Chaos and Complexity*, 263–87.

17 Peacocke, "God's Interaction with the World," 274.

18 Murphy, "Divine Action in the Natural Order," 339. (italics mine)

19 Dennis Bielfeldt, "Downward Causation: How Does the Mental Matter?" (Paper presented at the meeting of the European Society for the Study of Science and Theology, Lyon, France, April 18, 2000), 7.

20 Bielfeldt, "Downward Causation," 6.

21 Joseph LeDoux, *Synaptic Self: How Our Brains Become Who We Are* (New York: Penguin, 2003), 319.

22 See Dennis Bielfeldt, "Nancey Murphy's Nonreductive Physicalism," *Zygon* 34 (December 1999): 619–28; Nancey Murphy, "Theology and Science within a Lakatosian Program," *Zygon* 34 (December 1999): 629–42.

23 Murphy, "Divine Action in the Natural Order," 339.

24 Murphy, "Divine Action in the Natural Order," 339x.

25 Peacocke, "God's Interaction with the World," 286.

26 David Deutsch, "Quantum Computing," in *The New Humanists: Science at the Edge*, ed. John Brockman (New York: Barnes and Noble, 2003), 194.

27 Victor J. Stenger, *Has Science Found God? The Latest Results in the Search for Purpose in the Universe* (Amherst, N.Y.: Prometheus, 2003), 313.

28 See, especially, John Haught, *God After Darwin: A Theology of Evolution* (Boulder, Colo.: Westview, 2000), and "In Search of a God for Evolution: Paul Tillich and Pierre Teilhard de Chardin," *Zygon* 37 (2002): 539–553.

29 Gould uses the phrase in the conversations taped for television by Dutch journalist Wym Kyzer, conversations that take on book form in *A Glorious Accident*, ed. Wym Kyzer and Oliver Sacks (New York: W. H. Freeman, 1997).

30 Frederick Crews, "Saving Us from Darwin, Part II," *The New York Review of Books* XLVIII (October 18, 2001): 52.

31 Murphy, "Divine Action in the Natural Order," 341.

32 Murphy, "Divine Action in the Natural Order," 342.

33 Murphy, "Divine Action in the Natural Order," 342.

34 Kenneth R. Miller, *Finding Darwin's God: A Scientist's Search for Common Ground Between God and Evolution* (New York: HarperCollins, 1999), 241.

35 Jeffrey Koperski, "God, Chaos, and the Quantum Dice," *Zygon* 35 (September 2000): 557

36 Murphy, "Divine Action in the Natural Order," 356.

37 Murphy, "Theology and Science within a Lakatosian Program," 640.

38 Robert John Russell, "Divine Action and Quantum Mechanics: A Fresh Assessment," in *Quantum Mechanics: Scientific Perspectives on Divine Action*, vol. 5, ed. Robert John Russell, Philip Clayton, Kirk Wegter-McNelly, and John Polkinghorne (Vatican City State: Vatican Observatory Publications, and Berkeley: Center for Theology and the Natural Sciences, 2001), 299. See also George F. R. Ellis, "Quantum Theory and the Macroscopic World," Section 1.3, in *Quantum Mechanics*, 260–262.

39 See physicist Lisa Randall's observation that "Although a photoreceptor in an eye is sufficiently sensitive to perceive the smallest possible units of light—individual quanta—an eye typically processes so many quanta that any would-be quantum effects are overwhelmed by more readily apparent classical behavior."

Warped Passages: Unravelling the Mysteries of the Universe's Hidden Dimensions (New York: HarperCollins, 2005), 118.

40 William R. Stoeger, S. J., "Describing God's Action in the World in Light of Scientific Knowledge of Reality," in *Chaos and Complexity*, 242 n4.

41 "It's All Down to a Roll of the Dice," *New Scientist*, October 6–12, 2007, p. 14.

42 All biblical citations are from the *New Revised Standard Version*, National Council of the Churches of Christ in the United States of America, 1989.

43 For a helpful overview, see Brian Greene, *The Elegant Universe: Superstrings, Hidden Dimensions, and the Quest for the Ultimate Theory* (New York: Norton, 1999.

44 Greene, *The Elegant Universe*, 283 (emphasis mine). Note that, in 2003, the PBS series *Nova* adapted the highlights of Greene's book for a two-part television program. In the spirit of Talmudic debate, in which one sometimes happily supplies one's opponent with arguments just so that the search for truth can be pursued as effectively as possible, Greene's hint about unification theory pointing to the inevitability of the universe's structure and laws, might be supplied to the theist as an interesting counter to the problem of theodicy. If the theist can overcome the basic problem of inevitability erasing the need for a Designer—no small order—the notion of inevitability could be used against the problem of theodicy by pointing out that evil and suffering in the world do not count against the world having been created by a benevolent God. For the fact of the matter would be that this universe, including its evil and suffering, is not simply the Leibnizian "best of all possible worlds" but the *only possible world*. This line of argument springs to mind thanks to my freshman philosophy teacher, Professor Evan Fales. Though Fales was not (and presumably still is not) a theist, he thought the argument against theism based on theodicy was not airtight. In those days (the

mid-1970s), of course, philosophers were not talking much about the theory of everything and inevitability. Fales took a related approach, however. He suggested that the atheist who says that a benevolent God would have constructed a world without so much suffering and evil bears the burden of showing that such a world could, indeed, be built. But, of course, we have nothing even approaching the knowledge required to show that a universe with alternative laws could be constructed. As a concrete example of our inability to accomplish such a task, Fales pointed to our relative impotence in the face of the notorious Newtonian three-body problem.

45 Claudia Kalb, "Faith and Healing," *Newsweek,* November 10, 2003, 44–56. Unfortunately, the folks who put together the *cover* of the *Newsweek* issue in question could not quite resist the temptation to engage in the usual hype and even give a false impression about the conclusions reached inside the magazine: "God and Health: Is Religion Good Medicine? *Why Science Is Starting to Believe.*"

46 Kalb, "Faith and Healing," 48.

47 Kalb, "Faith and Healing," 49. A fourth group, that received a combination of prayer and music therapy, *did* have death rates 30 percent lower than patients in the other groups.

48 Benedict Carey, "Long-Awaited Medical Study Questions the Power of Prayer," *The New York Times*, March 31, 2006, 1.

49 Kalb, "Faith and Healing," 53.

50 The latest wrinkle in the "creationist" or "creation scientist" argument is what is called intelligent design theory, which focuses on issues such as information theory and complexity. Needless to say, the larger scientific community has found nothing of merit in intelligent design theory. For detailed refutations of its claims, see Taner Edis, "Darwin in Mind: 'Intelligent Design' Meets Artificial Intelligence," *Skeptical Inquirer*

25 (March/April 2001): 35–39; Robert T. Pennock, *Tower of Babel: The Evidence Against the New Creationism* (Cambridge: MIT, 2001); David Roche, "A Bit Confused: Creationism and Information Theory," *Skeptical Inquirer* 25 (March/April, 2001): 40–42. For a particularly succinct and helpful refutation, utilizing only a little higher mathematics (in the discussion of information theory), see Stenger, *Has Science Found God?*

51 See Owen Chadwick, *Newman* (New York: Oxford University Press, 1983), 49–50; 66.

52 Paul Tillich, *Dynamics of Faith* (New York: Harper and Row [Harper Torchbooks] 1957), 81.

53 Stephen Jay Gould, *Rocks of Ages: Science and Religion in the Fullness of Life* (New York: Ballantine, 1999), 4.

54 Gould, *Rocks of Ages*, 3.

55 Gould, *Rocks of Ages*, 213.

56 Gould, *Rocks of Ages*, 214.

57 For a potentially devastating analysis of how one theistic claim after another can be falsified by science, see Victor Stenger's *God: The Failed Hypothesis* (Amherst, N.Y.: Prometheus, 2007).

58 Andrew Newberg, Eugene D'Aquili, and Vince Rause, *Why God Won't Go Away: Brain Science and the Biology of Belief* (New York: Ballantine, 2002), 37. It should be pointed out that Newberg himself is much more optimistic about the possibility of harmonizing science and traditional religion than am I.

59 Gould, *Rocks of Ages*, 62.

60 See Gould, *Rocks of Ages*, 191–207.

61 Reported in Stenger, *Has Science Found God?*, 78.

62 For a more thorough attempt to show that science can actually falsify theism, see Stenger, *God: The Failed Hypothesis.*

63 Aristotle himself actually envisioned a host of "first movers," but Jewish, Christian, and Muslim monotheists saw fit to adapt his general notion for their own purposes.

64 "Hysterical Scientism: The Ecstasy of Richard Dawkins," \ *Harper's*, November 2006, 86.

65 Michael Brooks, "In Place of God: Can Secular Science Ever oust Religious Belief—and Should It Even Try?" *New Scientist*, November 18, 2006, 8–11.

66 Gary Wolf, "The New Atheism: No Heaven. No Hell. Just Science. Inside the Crusade against Religion," *Wired*, November 2006, 182–193.

Chapter 2

1 For a scholarly discussion of such practices among women, see Cynthia Eller, *Living in the Lap of the Goddess: The Feminist Spirituality Movement in America* (New York: Crossroad, 1993), chapter six.

2 Elizabeth Claire Prophet, Patricia R. Spadaro, and Murray L. Steinman, *Saint Germain's Prophecy for the New Millenium: Includes Dramatic Prophecies from Nostradamus, Edgar Cayce, and Mother Mary*, (Gardiner, Montana: Summit University Press, 1999).

3 Arlene Tognetti and Lisa Lenard, *The Complete Idiot's Guide to Tarot and Fortune-Telling*, (New York: Penguin, 1998).

4   Rio Olesky, *Astrology and Consciousness: The Wheel of Light*, (Tempe, Ariz.: New Falcon, 1996).

5   Doreen Virtue, *Archangels and Ascended Masters: A Guide to Working and Healing with Divinities and Deities*, (Carlsbad, Calif.: Hay House, 2003).

6   Edgar Cayce, *Auras: An Essay on the Meaning of Colors*, (Virginia Beach, Va.: A.R.E., 1991).

7   Kenneth Meadows, *Shamanic Experience: A Practical Guide to Psychic Powers*, (Rochester, Vt.: Inner Traditions, 2003).

8   Joshua David Store, *The Complete Ascension Manual for the Aquarian Age: How to Achieve Ascension in this Life-Time*, (Flagstaff, Ariz.: Light Technology, 1994).

9   Gillian Kemp, *The Dream Book: Dream Spells, Nighttime Potions and Riguals, and other Magical Sleep Formulas*, (London: Little, Brown, 2001).

10   Mary Daly, *Outercourse: The Be-Dazzling Voyage* (San Francisco: HarperSanFrancisco, 1992), 208.

11   Lindbeck's major work is *The Nature of Doctrine: Religion and Theology in a Postliberal Age* (Philadelphia: Westminster, 1984). It is usually agreed that the founding work of left-wing postmodern theology is Mark C. Taylor's *Erring: A Postmodern A/Theology* (Chicago: University of Chicago, 1984). See also Edith Wyschogrod, *Saints and Postmodernism: Revisioning Moral Philosophy* (Chicago: University of Chicago, 1990); Charles E. Winquist, *Desiring Theology* (Chicago: University of Chicago, 1995); Graham Ward, ed., *The Postmodern God: A Theological Reader* (Malden, Mass.: Blackwell, 1997); Clayton Crockett, ed., *Secular Theology: American Radical Theological Thought* (London: Routledge, 2001).

12 Jean François Lyotard, *The Postmodern Condition: A Report on Knowledge*, trans. Geoff Benington and Brian Massumi (Minneapolis: University of Minnesota, 1984), xxiv.

13 See, for example, Victor Stenger, *God: The Failed Hypothesis* (Amherst, N.Y.: Prometheus, 2007), 39, 132.

14 Quoted in Alan Sokal and Jean Bricmont, *Fashionable Nonsense: Postmodern Intellectuals' Abuse of Science* (New York: Picador, 1998), 184.

15 Sokal and Bricmont, *Fashionable Nonsense*, 46.

16 Taylor, *Erring*, 21. The quotation is from Francis Bacon.

17 See Rosemary Radford Ruether, *Sexism and God-Talk: Toward a Feminist Theology* (Boston: Beacon, 1983).

18 Rosemary Radford Ruether, *Gaia and God: An Ecofeminist Theology of Earth Healing* (San Francisco: HarperSanFrancisco, 1992).

19 Ruether, *Gaia and God*, 4.

20 Ruether, *Gaia and God*, 47.

21 See Ruether, *Gaia and God*, 36–40.

22 Ruether, *Gaia and God*, 195.

23 Sallie McFague, *The Body of God: An Ecological Theology* (Minneapolis: Fortress, 1993).

24 Ruether, *Gaia and God*, 57.

Chapter 3

1 My treatments here of McFague, Daly, Kaufman, and Good-enough are based on my earlier book, *Gods After God: An Introduction to Contemporary Radical Theologies* (New York: State University of New York Press, 2006). In that book, I provide a more thorough treatment of these thinkers. Not surprisingly, I focus in the present study simply on what these theologians have to say that is relevant to science.

2 Sallie McFague, *Models of God: Theology for an Ecological, Nuclear Age* (Philadelphia: Fortress, 1987), x.

3 Sallie McFague, *Metaphorical Theology: Models of God in Religious Language* (Philadelphia: Fortress, 1982), x.

4 McFague, *Models of God*, xi.

5 McFague, *Models of God*, xiii.

6 McFague, *Metaphorical Theology*, 101.

7 On this all-important set of metaphors and models see, in addition to the works cited above, McFague's *The Body of God: An Ecological Theology* (Minneapolis: Augsburg Fortress, 1993) and *Super, Natural Christians: How We Should Love Nature* (Minneapolis: Augsburg Fortress, 1997).

8 McFague, *The Body of God*, 145.

9 McFague, *The Body of God*, 181.

10 Mary Daly, *Outercourse: The Be-Dazzling Voyage* (San Francisco: HarperSanFrancisco, 1992), 326.

11 Mary Daly, *Pure Lust: Elemental Femmist Philosophy*, (Boston: Beacon Press, 1984), 400.

12 Mary Daly, *Quintessence . . . Realizing the Archaic Future* (Boston: Beacon Press, 1998), 54.

13 Mary Daly, *Gyn/Ecology: The Metaethics of Radical Feminism* (Boston: Beacon Press, 1978), 23.

14 Mary Daly, with Jane Caputi, *Webster's First New Intergalactic Wickedary of the English Language* (Boston: Beacon Press, 1987), 96.

15 Elsewhere. I have attempted to work out in detail an enactment model or interpretation of feminist theology. See my *When God Becomes Goddess: The Transformation of American Religion* (New York: Continuum, 1995).

16 Mary Daly, *Quintessence*, 54.

17 Gordon Kaufman, *God—Mystery—Diversity: Christian Theology in a Pluralistic World* (Minneapolis: Fortress, 1996), 180.

18 Recall, for instance, that Aquinas' use of analogy in talking about God is supremely realistic. When I say that Anita is loving and God is loving, my concept of love is borrowed from the sort of love I see practiced by Anita, that is, finite, human love. Divine love is merely analogous to Anita's love. I think of it as *like* Anita's love but as purged of all the limitations of human love. Yet, the term *love* applies, for Thomas, more exactly and more literally to God than it does to Anita, for God's love is perfect love, indeed, the very epitome of love.

19 Gordon Kaufman, *The Theological Imagination: Constructing the Concept of God* (Philadelphia: Westminister, 1981), 16.

20 Kaufman, *The Theological Imagination*, 32. In the quotation cited, which is from a relatively early book, Kaufman says that this construction sums up our ideals in a "personification." But in his later work, he decides that our God-concept really ought not be personal, since the only forms of personality that we know are derived from biological evolution.

21 Kaufman, *In Face of Mystery: A Constructive Theology* (Cambridge: Harvard University Press, 1993), 308.

22 Kaufman, *God—Mystery—Diversity*, 102.

23 See Kaufman, *In the Face of Mystery*, chapter 17.

24 Kaufman, *In Face of Mystery*, 232.

25 In my exposition of Kaufman here, I have been careful to speak consistently of Kaufman's construction of the *concept* of God. Unfortunately, Kaufman himself is inconsistent in a way that can lead to significant ambiguity in his work. He can use the terms *concept, metaphor* and *image*, interchangeably (see for example, Kaufman, *In Face of Mystery*, 43.). This is highly problematic, in that a symbol or metaphor, following Paul Ricouer, presents a first-level meaning that breaks down in a significant contradiction—God cannot really be a mother, lacking as God does the requisite physiological equipment—so that we are forced to look for a second level of meaning—God is *like* a mother in certain specific respects. See Paul Ricoeur, *Interpretation Theory: Discourse and the Surplus of Meaning* (Fort Worth: Texas Christian University, 1976). But to construct a *concept* of God by linking the word "God," suggesting that which is our ultimate object of devotion, with the evolutionary process that has resulted in human beings is to proceed in a very different fashion: the concept of the evolutionary process that leads to *Homo Sapiens* does not break down on a first level and thereby point us to a second level of meaning. At the same time—and this is an important qualification—there *is* in Kaufman's constructions a significant element of the "is-and-is-not" characteristic of metaphor and symbol. Kaufman's attaching the word "God," our ultimate object of devotion, to the concept of the evolutionary process is fraught, as we have seen, with existential mystery and risk. We assert that the evolutionary process that produced human beings is legitimately our ultimate reference point, our "God," but we cannot be sure that this decision is the correct one. Perhaps the evolutionary dynamic cannot, in fact, provide the existential meaning and direction that we seek. There is both commitment—the "is"—and a risk and uncertainty that mean that our assertions about God cannot be taken as unambiguous—the "is not."

26 The fear of nuclear apocalypse may appear outdated now that the Cold War is a thing of the past, but one could surely argue that the nuclear threat has returned in a new form: we now fear a nuclear attack from so-called "rogue nations," and we worry about a nuclear suitcase planted in a major urban center by terrorists. Indeed, some of us are holding our breath in the hope that the United States itself does not decide to employ nuclear weapons against a nation such as Iran.

27 See Rudolf Otto, *The Idea of the Holy: An Inquiry into the Non-Rational Factor in the Idea of the Divine and Its Relation to the Rational*, trans. John W. Harvey (New York: Oxford, 1958).

28 Ursula Goodenough, *The Sacred Depths of Nature* (New York: Oxford University Press, 1998), 9.

29 An example is provided by Mark C. Taylor's contention in *Erring* that we should invest the postmodernist notion of the productive milieu of language with ultimacy.

30 Goodenough, *The Sacred Depths of Nature*, 46.

31 Goodenough, *The Sacred Depths of Nature*, 64.

32 Goodenough, *The Sacred Depths of Nature*, 73.

33 Goodenough, *The Sacred Depths of Nature*, 50.

34 Goodenough, *The Sacred Depths of Nature*, 59.

35 Goodenough, *The Sacred Depths of Nature*, 47.

36 Lest one think that calling the universe, taken as a whole, *God*, and seeing self-conscious participation in it as a genuinely "religious" undertaking unduly stretches the use of the term *religion*, it should be noted that the dynamic of participation and self-transcendence that is central to our case for the universe is also central in those endeavors that we commonly label the "world *religions*." Hinduism seeks to transcend the phenomenal ego and participate in the Atman, the deep self that is

one with Brahman, the Godhead. Buddhism seeks a radical self-transcendence that regards the finite self as illusion and offers participation in nirvana. Taoism invites me to participate in the infinite Tao and overcome the prodding of the ego. Judaism looks for meaning through participation in a community and a God that far transcends the individual. Christ asks us to lose the ordinary self, to be "born again" in an act of radical transcendence that allows us to participate in the Kingdom of God. The very term *Islam* means submission: we are to submit the self to Allah in a disciplined act of participation and self-transcendence.

37 See Friedrich Schleirmacher, *The Christian Faith*, trans. ed. H. R. Mackintosh and J. S. Stewart (Philadelphia: Fortress, 1976). Schleiermacher's full formulation is the "immediate self-consciousness of absolute dependence." Now, on the one hand, my sense of dependence on the Big Bang is neither *immediate* nor suggestive of *absolute* dependence. It is mediated by the theories of contemporary cosmology. However, my sense of having some freedom over all of the individual entities in the universe but of being absolutely dependent over against the sheer fact that there is anything at all is, one may argue, indeed immediate. To the degree that the Big Bang explains how everything that is came into being, one might claim that contemplation of the Big Bang is a reflection upon my immediate self-consciousness of absolute dependence on the sheer fact of there being anything at all. Second, while the Big Bang is an extraordinary event, it is still, technically speaking, one event among others. And, therefore, while I experience mostly a sense of dependence over against it, I do perhaps have a small degree of freedom too, such as the freedom to conceptualize it. But once again, this may be a function of the fact that, while our conceptions of the Big Bang event and of what it actually involved—spontaneous symmetry-breaking, for example— may suggest one event among others, to the degree that the concept of the Big Bang explains why if there is anything at all, it is simply an explication of what is, in fact, something upon which we are absolutely dependent. The properly religious or

theological character of the Big Bang does not hinge, of course, upon whether it happens to be describable in the particular vocabulary of the "immediate self-consciousness of absolute dependence" employed by Schleiermacher.

38 See John Dewey, *A Common Faith* (New Haven, Yale University Press, 1934).

39 See Alan Ryan, *John Dewey and the High Tide of American Liberalism* (New York: Norton, 1995).

Chapter 4

1 For a provocative treatment of the anthropic principle, one that takes advantage of years of discussion about it among cosmologists, see Leonard Susskind, *The Cosmic Landscape: String Theory and the Illusion of Intelligent Design* (New York: Back Bay Books, 2006).

2 See Peter D. Ward and Donald Brownlee, *Rare Earth: Why Complex Life is Uncommon in the Universe* (New York: Copernicus, 2000).

3 See Christopher J. Conselice, "The Universe's Invisible Hand," *Scientific American*, February 2007, 35–41.

4 "Anecdote of the Jar," in *The Palm at the End of the Mind: Selected Poems and a Play*, ed. Holly Stevens (New York: Vintage, 1972), 46.

5 Of course, we cannot rule out the possibility that there are extraterrestrial consciousnesses that contribute a teleological dimension as well.

6 See Richard Dawkins, *The God Delusion* (Boston: Houghton Mifflin, 2006).

7 Hans-Georg Gadamer, *Truth and Method*, trans. and ed. Garrett Barden and John Cumming (New York: *Continuum*, 1975), 102.

8 There is perhaps something ironic about using Gadamer in this context, in that his concern is precisely to call into question the priority given to the sort of knowledge provided by methodical disciplines, the natural sciences in particular, when our whole enterprise is predicated upon the highest possible valuation of the knowledge that the natural sciences offer. Irony, however, does not equal contradiction here.

9 My example of the trees suggest a landscape painting so that the subject matter of the painting is a reflection of actual trees in the real world. This makes it fairly easy to see how the painting could tie into my project of participation in the universe. But even in the case of abstract or nonrepresentational art, the same dynamic can be at work. After all, that style of art still reflects genuine aspects of the real universe, such as color and geometry.

10 For an argument as to why, even in a radical theology, we ought to hold to the Christian tradition's claim that Jesus is "God," as well as to some of its other contentions, see my *Imaginary Christs: The Challenge of Christological Pluralism* (New York: SUNY, 2000).

Chapter 5

1 For a useful collection of such cosmogonies, see Barbara C. Sproul, *Primal Myths: Creating the World* (San Francisco: Harper and Row, 1979).

2 That ancient cosmogonies could be recognized even by some of their early adherents as symbolic rather than merely literal is evident by the fact that the Hebrew Bible/Old Testament

contains two quite different creation stories (see Gen. 1:1–31 and Gen. 2:4–23). If the editors of Genesis wished to claim literal accuracy for their account of the origins of the world, one presumes that they would not have included two different cosmogonies with significantly different details.

3 I borrow the term from Paul Ricouer, who uses it in the different context of textual interpretation. See *Interpretation Theory Discourse and the Surplus of Meaning* (Fort Worth: Texas Christian University, 1976), 43.

4 See Michio Kaku, *Parallel Worlds: A Journey Through Creation, Higher Dimensions, and the Future of the Cosmos.* (New York: Doubleday, 2005), 176–177.

5 Olivia Judson, "Why I'm Happy I Evolved," Week in Review, *The New York Times,* January 1, 2006, 8.

6 For a contemporary introduction to string/membrane theory, see Lisa Randall, *Warped Passages: Unraveling the Mysteries of the Universe's Hidden Dimensions* (New York: HarperCollins, 2005). On loop quantum gravity, see Lee Smolin, *Three Roads to Quantum Gravity* (New York: Basic Books, 2001), and "Atoms of Space and Time," *Scientific American* 290 (January 2004): 66–75. See also Smolin's critique of string theory, *The Trouble with Physics: The Rise of String Theory, The Fall of a Science, and What Comes Next* (Boston: Houghton Mifflin, 2006).

7 Stephen W. Hawking, *A Brief History of Time: From the Big Bang to Black Holes* (New York: Bantam, 1988), 175.

8 Carl Sagan, "Introduction," in Stephen Hawking, *A Brief History of Time,* x.

9 For a particularly engaging account of the implications of the multiverse idea, see Leonard Susskind, *The Cosmic Landscape: String Theory and the Illusion of Intelligent Design* (New York: Little, Brown, and Company, 2006).

10 This existential payoff of divine Oneness is well described in Huston Smith's textbook, *The World's Religions* (San Francisco: HarperCollins, 1991), 272–276.

11 Ursula Goodenough and Paul Woodruff, "Mindful Virtue, Mindful Reverence," *Zygon* 36 (December 2001): 585–595.

12 Goodenough and Woodruff, "Mindful Virtue, Mindful Reverence," 586.

13 Goodenough and Woodruff, "Mindful Virtue, Mindful Reverence," 586.

14 Goodenough and Woodruff, "Mindful Virtue, Mindful Reverence," 587 (emphasis mine).

15 Goodenough and Woodruff, "Mindful Virtue, Mindful Reverence," 588.

16 Brian Greene, *The Fabric of the Cosmos: Space, Time, and the Texture of Reality* (New York: Knopf, 2004), 21.

Chapter 6

1 Nancey Murphy and George F. R. Ellis, *On the Moral Nature of the Universe: Theology, Cosmology, and Ethics* (Minneapolis: Fortress, 1996).

2 Brian Greene, *The Fabric of the Cosmos: Space, Time, and the Texture of Reality* (New York: Knopf, 2004), p. 5.

3 Murphy and Ellis, *On the Moral Nature of the Universe*, 61.

4 Cf. Elizabeth A. Johnson, "Does God Play Dice? Divine Providence and Chance," *Theological Studies* 57 (1996): 3–18.

5 Murphy and Ellis, *On the Moral Nature of the Universe*, xv.

6 There is a third alternative to the proposals offered by Murphy and Ellis on the one hand and myself on the other: Murphy and Ellis want to unify our sense of the world through an intellectually mandated metaphysical theology. I have suggested that unity can come from voluntary adoption of a scientifically informed pantheism. But scientist Edward O. Wilson splits the difference by arguing that our knowledge of the world can be unified via an intellectually mandated route, but that the intellectual road map to unity need not involve any description of transcendent territory. Science itself can produce unity, can achieve "consilience." See Edward O. Wilson, *Consilience: The Unity of Knowledge* (New York: Random House, 1999); and Edward O. Wilson, "Back from Chaos," *The Atlantic Monthly* 281 (March, 1998): 41–62.

7 Ray Kurzweil, *The Age of Spiritual Machines: When Computers Exceed Human Intelligence* (New York: Penguin, 1999), 73.

8 See David Chalmers, "Facing Up to Consciousness," *Exploring Consciousness*, ed. Rita Carter (Berkeley: University of California, 2002), 50.

9 See Dan Lloyd, *Radiant Cool: A Novel Theory of Consciousness* (Cambridge, Mass.: MIT Press, 2004).

10 Kurzweil, *The Age of Spiritual Machines*, 64.

11 Kurzweil, *The Age of Spiritual Machines*, 63.

12 See Roger Penrose, *The Emperor's New Mind* (New York: Penguin, 1989), and *Shadows of the Mind: A Search for the Missing Science of Consciousness* (Oxford: Oxford University Press, 1994).

13 Murphy's and Ellis' discussion of free will is sophisticated and insightful, but note that, at the end of the day, they must simply posit the existence of free will since science has not yet offered the tools to uncover its possibility. See Murphy and Ellis,

On the Moral Nature of the Universe, 32–37. My hunch on this topic is that science will eventually demonstrate that we possess "finite freedom" (the phrase is Paul Tillich's, but not the conceptuality). That is, since the indeterminate character of individual quantum phenomena is moot where human action is concerned due to the predictable behavior of those phenomena in aggregate on the macro-level, human beings are, in fact, determined by a host of complex forces, including genetic heritage, natural environment, and social environment. But I nonetheless experience myself as free, and rightly so, for the unique, incomprehensibly intricate collective product of those genetic, environmental, and other forces is just what I mean by my identity. My actions, in other words, are determined by the unity of a host of factors, which unity I experience as my identity. I am free, albeit within limits, hence, I have "finite freedom." What is relevant for our purposes is that, while it is not clear that such limited freedom could be squared with traditional theistic notions of moral and religious responsibility, this kind of freedom could in fact be productively harmonized with the sort of participation and self-transcendence at issue in what I am calling a scientifically informed pantheism.

14 See Andy Clark, *Natural-Born Cyborgs: Minds, Technologies, and the Future of Human Intelligence* (Oxford: Oxford University, 2003), and Kurzweil, *The Age of Spiritual Machines.*

15 See Anselm of Canterbury, "Concerning Truth," in *Truth, Freedom, and Evil: Three Philosophical Dialogues*, ed. and trans. Jasper Hopkins and Herbert Richardson (New York: Harper and Row, 1967), 91–120.

16 For a contemporary philosophical analysis of the connection between the notion of centered selfhood and the being of God, see Taylor, *Erring: A Postmodern A/Theology* (Chicago: University of Chicago, 1984).

17 *Basic Writings of Saint Augustine*, 2 vols., ed. Whitney J. Oates (New York: Random House, 1948), 1:3.

Chapter 7

1 One of the world's most significant post-industrial nations, Japan, has no significant history of Christian theism. Yet, it is following the Western pattern of secularization, with young adults in Japan today thinking of religion as something that their grandparents practice.

2 See Daniel C. Dennett, *Breaking the Spell: Religion as a Natural Phenomenon* (New York: Viking, 2006).

INDEX